Courtship

**SAGE SERIES ON
CLOSE RELATIONSHIPS**

Series Editors
Clyde Hendrick, Ph.D., and
Susan S. Hendrick, Ph.D.

Courtship

Rodney M. Cate
Sally A. Lloyd

Sage
Series
on Close
Relationships

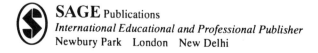
SAGE Publications
International Educational and Professional Publisher
Newbury Park   London   New Delhi

For information address:

SAGE Publications, Inc.
2455 Teller Road
Newbury Park, California 91320

SAGE Publications Ltd.
6 Bonhill Street
London EC2A 4PU
United Kingdom

SAGE Publications India Pvt. Ltd.
M-32 Market
Greater Kailash I
New Delhi 110 048 India

Printed in the United States of America

Library of Congress Cataloging-in-Publication Data

Cate, Rodney M.
    Courtship / Rodney M. Cate, Sally A. Lloyd
        p.   cm. —(Sage series on close relationships)
    Includes bibliographical references and index.
    ISBN 0-8039-3708-3 (cl). —ISBN 0-8039-3709-1 (pb)
    1. Courtship—United States. 2. Dating (Social customs)
I. Lloyd, Sally A. II. Title. III. Series.
HQ801.C34   1992
306.73'4—dc20   92-5751

92 93 94 95 10 9 8 7 6 5 4 3 2

Sage Production Editor: Diane S. Foster

Contents

Series Editors' Introduction

When we first began our work on love attitudes more than a decade ago, we did not know what to call our research area. In some ways it represented an extension of earlier work in interpersonal attraction. Most of our scholarly models were psychologists (though sociologists had long been deeply involved in the areas of courtship and marriage), yet we sometimes felt as if our work had no professional "home." That has all changed. Our research not only has a home, it has an extended family as well, and the family is composed of relationship researchers. Over the past decade the discipline of close relationships (also called personal relationships and intimate relationships) has emerged, developed, and flourished.

Two aspects of close relationships research should be noted. The first is its rapid growth, resulting in numerous books, journals, handbooks, book series, and professional organizations. As fast as the field grows, however, the demand for even more research and knowledge seems to be ever increasing. Questions about close, personal relationships still far exceed answers. The second noteworthy aspect of the new discipline of close relationships is its interdisciplinary nature. The field owes its vitality to scholars from communications, family studies and human development, psychology (clinical, counseling, developmental, social), and sociology as well as other disciplines such as nursing and social work. It is this interdisciplinary wellspring that gives close relationships research its diversity and richness, qualities that we hope to achieve in the current series.

The Sage Series on Close Relationships is designed to acquaint diverse readers with the most up-to-date information about various topics in close relationships theory and research. Each volume in the series covers a particular topic or theme in one area of close relationships. Each book reviews the particular topic area, describes contemporary research in the area (including the authors' own work, where appropriate), and offers some suggestions for interesting research questions and/or real-world applications related to the topic. The volumes are designed to be appropriate for students and professionals in communication, family studies, psychology, sociology, and social work, among others. A basic assumption of the series is that the broad panorama of close relationships can best be portrayed by authors from multiple disciplines so that the series cannot be "captured" by any single disciplinary bias.

The current volume, *Courtship*, deals with relationship development, a process that must be understood if we are ever to be more knowledgeable about close relationships. Rodney Cate and Sally Lloyd have reviewed a wealth of scholarship relevant to courtship and relationship development, giving us a historical understanding of courtship in the United States and presenting contemporary research that variously portrays both the ongoing nature of relationship development and the pain that can result when courtship goes awry. In many ways relationship development is the fortune teller's crystal ball for predicting a relationship's future.

CLYDE HENDRICK
SUSAN S. HENDRICK
SERIES EDITORS

Preface

Our view of courtship is one that acknowledges that close relationships evolve through the interaction of their participants as well as being embedded in and reciprocally tied to various contexts (historical, social network, physical environment, etc.). Consequently, this volume uses the work of sociologists, family scientists, communications specialists, and psychologists. We also are defining the concept of "courtship" rather broadly. The concept includes relationships that move to marriage as well as those that end before marriage and might more accurately be called "dating" relationships in that there may be no present intent to marry. Our assumption is that knowledge concerning "dating" relationships will inform us about the dynamics of these relationships and the movement to marriage.

The six chapters of this book vary from historical descriptions of courtship to the scientific study of the phenomenon. Chapter 1 makes the case that the study of courtship is important because the premarital phase of relationships may significantly affect the later course of marriage. The chapter outlines background, personality, and dyadic characteristics that may operate premaritally to affect later marriage and presents empirical research that substantiates the important role of these factors.

Chapter 2 traces the historical roots of courtship in America. Although early American courtship held on to vestiges of its European heritage, a participant-run system of courtship developed quite soon after the colonies were established. The chapter characterizes the essential features of this participant-run courtship system during specific eras of America's history.

Chapter 3 discusses various models of courtship that have guided research in this area over the past 40 years. Early models of courtship were static in nature and assumed that a similar set of factors influenced mate choice for all premarital couples. Such factors as attitude similarity, value consensus, social similarity, and personality complementarity were postulated to propel people to marriage. Later models assumed that there was a sequential set of factors that progressively narrowed the potential pool of mates until an appropriate mate was found. The chapter presents an alternative to these sequential models, the interpersonal process model. This model assumes that the course of courtship is affected by different levels of causes, particularly the unique interaction of partners.

Chapter 4 reviews the major longitudinal studies of premarital relationship stability that have occurred since 1970. This review examines the individual, dyadic, social network, and circumstantial factors that have been found to discriminate between stable and unstable premarital relationships. Nearly all of the factors examined do successfully discriminate between stable and unstable relationships. When compared with each other, however, few of the factors are consistently unique predictors of stability.

Chapter 5 focuses on the "dark side" of courtship. We first present studies that have attempted to identify static factors that predict premarital breakup over a relatively short period of time. Next the chapter explores the processes that are involved in the dissolution phase of premarital relationships. The second part of the chapter deals with physical and sexual abuse in premarital relationships. We outline the incidence of such abuse, its correlates at several levels of analysis, and the impact of this abuse. A conceptual model of the "dark side of courtship" is then proposed.

In Chapter 6 we present our thoughts on the future of courtship research and on the future of courtship itself. We discuss various research and theory needs that are suggested by current models of courtship development. Last, we speculate about the likely future changes that may come about in the institution of courtship.

RODNEY M. CATE
SALLY A. LLOYD

1

Introduction:
The Importance of Courtship

Over and over again both professional and popular authors raise the question "Is Marriage Dead?" As early as 1927 John Watson predicted that the institution of marriage would be "kaput" in 50 years (Watson, 1927). Other authors throughout this century have reiterated this hue and cry, lamenting the inexorable effect of rapid social change on the family. Despite the dire predictions, the institution of marriage has survived rather well through the last decade of the twentieth century.

In fact, in many ways marriage is as popular as ever. The United States currently has one of the highest ever-married rates among developed nations (Glick, 1984). It is projected (Glick, 1984) that at least 96% of individuals from the 1930-1939 birth cohort will marry at some point in their lives. The projections are slightly lower for later birth cohorts; for example, individuals of marriageable age during the 1980s (i.e., 25 to 29 year olds) are expected to have a marriage rate of 88% for women and 90% for men (Glick, 1984). Despite the long-term trend of decreasing marriage rates across the twentieth century (Mintz & Kellogg, 1988), the vast majority of Americans do indeed marry.

Most people who marry do so in the context of "until death do us part" and "happily ever after" (Skolnick, 1987). Unfortunately, the projected divorce rate of 50% (Glick, 1984) can only lead to the conclusion that "happily ever after" is a particularly difficult state to achieve. Many scholars have attempted to address the reasons for our high divorce rate and the prevalence of unhappiness in marriage. Given that the breakdown of marriage occurs for many couples in the very early years of marriage (the average length of marriage before separation is only 5 years; Cherlin, 1981), many marital problems most likely have their roots in the premarital stage. Premarital partners often have some inkling of what is to come in marriage (both good and bad), but because of the romanticized nature of courtship, partners are able to ignore the bad and glorify the good (Lloyd, 1991).

We believe that courtship sets the foundation for the later quality and stability of marriage (Cate & Lloyd, 1988; Lloyd & Cate, 1985b). Many of the processes considered important for marital success (e.g., positive communication, ability to successfully resolve conflict) are likely developed during the courtship phase, often long before the decision to marry has been made. Our understanding of marriage is at best incomplete without a thorough understanding of the forces that influence the early (i.e., premarital) development of the marital relationship. Courtship is, after all, the first (and perhaps most crucial) stage of the family life cycle (Lloyd & Cate, 1985b).

❧ Predicting Marital Success From Premarriage Factors

Some of the earliest research on courtship undertaken by family studies scholars examined the power of premarriage factors in predicting later marital success (e.g., Adams, 1946; Burgess & Cottrell,

1939; Terman & Buttenweiser, 1938). These studies emphasized the role of background factors and personality in later marital happiness. Over time the focus of such predictive studies shifted from characteristics of the individual to dyadic factors (Wamboldt & Reiss, 1989). This shift from individual to dyadic factors parallels the corresponding shift in the history of courtship from "choosing a quality person" to "enhancing the quality of the relationship."

The Role of Background Factors

Many background factors have been studied in relation to marital success, most notably, age at marriage, length of courtship, education, and quality of the childhood environment. Marital success is typically defined in two ways: as marital happiness and/or as marital stability.

Age at marriage has been consistently shown to be related to marital instability (Booth, Johnson, White, & Edwards, 1987). Teenage marriages are particularly prone to divorce (Kitson, Barbi, & Roach, 1985), and to a smaller extent, individuals marrying after age 30 are more prone to divorce than are individuals marrying in their 20s (Norton & Glick, 1979). The impact of age at marriage on divorce, however, is almost entirely limited to young people and marriages of short duration (Booth et al., 1987). Generally young marriages that end in divorce are likely to do so within 5 years.

The relationship between age at marriage and marital happiness is also consistent (although most of the studies that have examined this relationship are rather dated). The older the members of the couple at marriage, the higher the level of marital happiness (Burgess & Cottrell, 1939; Burgess & Wallin, 1953; Burr, 1973; Lewis & Spanier, 1979; Terman, 1938). Burr (1973) noted that this relationship is largely a function of young age at marriage; as the spouses' ages at marriage approach the mid-twenties, the relationship between age at marriage and marital happiness levels off.

Length of courtship is positively related to marital adjustment (Lewis & Spanier, 1979). Partners who have dated for longer periods of time and who have been engaged longer report higher marital happiness (Burgess & Wallin, 1953; Locke, 1951; Spanier, 1971). Longer courtships are believed to allow partners the time to test their compatibility and gain important information about one another (Cate & Lloyd, 1988). It is possible, however, for a courtship to be "too long." Huston (in preparation) has demonstrated that long, troubled courtships characterized by a slow acceleration of commitment and numerous downturns are predictive of lower marital happiness and increased divorce.

Level of education is related to both marital adjustment and stability (Burgess & Wallin, 1953; Burr, 1973; Kitson et al., 1985; Kurdek, 1991). Lewis and Spanier (1979) have conceptualized level of education, age at marriage, and length of courtship as "premarital resources"; such resources are believed to contribute to "adequate role functioning" in marriage. We have noted previously (Cate & Lloyd, 1988) that these findings support the idea that premarital processes are related to later marital success. Unfortunately the specific nature of the key premarital processes remains unspecified in these studies.

Quality of the childhood environment is also positively related to marital adjustment. Happiness in one's parents' marriage, greater attachment to parents and siblings, lower childhood conflict with parents, and firm discipline are all associated with greater adjustment in one's own marriage (Adams, 1946; Burgess & Wallin, 1953; Kelly & Conley, 1987; Terman, 1938; Terman & Buttenweiser, 1938). There may be a gender difference in this relationship, however. Vaillant (1978) reported that the quality of the childhood environment was unrelated to marital happiness in his longitudinal study of men. Others have shown (Wamboldt & Reiss, 1989) that it is the wife's positive relationship with the family of origin, rather than the husband's, that is a key factor in later marital happiness. Indeed, in some cases, overly close ties between the husband and his family of origin predicted lesser marital satisfaction.

Many of the longitudinal studies of background factors and marital happiness are somewhat dated. Most of these studies have examined marriages that began between 1930 and 1950 (e.g., Adams, 1946; Burgess & Wallin, 1953; Kelly & Conley, 1987; Sears, 1977; Vaillant, 1978). It is not entirely clear whether similar findings would emerge from longitudinal studies of marriages from later cohorts, especially given the significant changes in the social context of marriage that have occurred from the 1960s to the present (e.g., rise in the divorce rate, decreased fertility).

The intergenerational transmission of divorce is a case in point. A positive association between parental divorce and one's own divorce probability has been consistently noted by several scholars (Bumpass & Sweet, 1972; Mueller & Pope, 1977; White, 1990) although the association is small. Other scholars have failed to support the inter-generational transmission hypothesis altogether (e.g., Hanson & Tuch, 1984). Booth, Brinkerhoff and White (1984) more directly analyzed the impact of parental divorce on courtship. They found that ado-lescents who had experienced parental divorce reported more court-ship activity (e.g., dated more often) and less satisfaction with their courtship relationships than adolescents from intact families; this was especially true if the divorce had been accompanied by hostility between the parents and an increase in parent-child conflict, and if the custodial parent remained single. Booth et al. (1984) noted that it is not clear at this time whether individuals of marriageable age in the 1980s are affected adversely by parental divorce (e.g., have less commitment to marriage or inadequate skills for dealing with conflict) or positively (e.g., are determined not to repeat their parents' mistakes).

Whether older age at marriage, greater length of courtship, greater education and childhood happiness represent a "maturity" factor or a "premarital skill" factor may be a moot point. It is clear, however, that background characteristics of the individual have an impact on both the course of premarital relationship development and the course of the marriage. At the very least the interplay of parental role models, interpersonal skills, and readiness for marriage be-tween the two members of the developing dyad have an important influence on both courtship and marriage.

Personality Factors

Scholars have long been fascinated with the relationship between personality and marital happiness. Starting with the work of Terman (1938), a succession of studies (both longitudinal and cross-sectional) have assessed the impact of traits such as neuroticism, emotional stability, and conventionality on marital satisfaction and stability. We limit our review of these studies to longitudinal works that assessed personality premaritally or in the very earliest stages of the marriage.

Three longitudinal studies are striking in their long durations. Vaillant (1978) assessed a sample of college men in the 1930s. Forty years later he assessed marital stability and satisfaction of 51 of these men and found that maritally satisfied men had been rated as significantly more mentally healthy (versus mentally ill) in college than were subsequently divorced or maritally dissatisfied men. Both Sears (1977) and Terman and Oden (1947) reported similar results from Terman's longitudinal study of more than 500 gifted children. A measure of the emotional stability of the gifted children at ages 7-14 predicted marital happiness nearly two decades later; in addition, the Terman marital aptitude test, which assessed both family background and neuroticism of personality, predicted both marital happiness and stability. Kelly and Conley (1987) conducted another long-term longitudinal study of marital success. They first assessed 300 engaged couples in the 1930s and most recently reassessed 200 of the couples in the 1980s. They found strong support for the predictive power of personality; husbands' marital adjustment was predicted by lower neuroticism, higher impulse control, and greater conventionality, and wives' adjustment was predicted by lower neuroticism, higher impulse control and greater conformity to social ideals.

Four short-term longitudinal studies bear mention as well. Adams (1946) conducted a longitudinal study of 100 engaged couples; he reassessed the couples between the second and third year of marriage. His results demonstrated that premarital assessments of tranquility, frankness and steadiness of the men and frankness, stability, and contentedness of the women predicted marital happiness. Burgess and Wallin (1953), in a 5-year longitudinal study of 1,000 engaged couples, noted that premarital levels of emotional stability, consideration for others, companionableness, self-confidence, and emotional dependency predicted later marital happiness. Finally, Bentler and Newcomb (1978) conducted a 4-year longitudinal study of 162 newly married couples. For men, less extraversion and more deliberateness correlated with later marital adjustment, and less extraversion, invulnerability, and orderliness correlated with later divorce. For women, less ambition, less art interest, less intelligence, greater objectivity, and greater stability correlated with later marital adjustment, whereas less congeniality correlated with divorce. Homogamy of attractiveness, extraversion, and art interest also correlated with marital stability. Finally, Kurdek (1991) studied 402 engaged couples through their first year of marriage. He found that similarity of attachment, motivation to be in the relationship, social support, expressiveness and psychological distress differentiated intact from separated couples over time.

In some sense a discussion of how personality traits predict marital success seems hardly related to our argument that processes established in courtship set the stage for marital happiness. Such an *intrapersonal* model, which emphasizes the role of particular personality traits in causing later marital problems, appears rather immutable and hardly compatible with an *interpersonal* model, which emphasizes the role of dysfunctional marital interaction (Kelly & Conley, 1987). Kelly and Conley (1987) noted, however, that the two models are not mutually exclusive, for the interpersonal model may explain the process by which the intrapersonal model works. Blumstein and Kollock (1988) went a step further by asserting that personality traits and patterns of interaction are ultimately inseparable: "love or dominance are features of relationships, not individuals; no person is loving, compatible or domineering in an interpersonal vacuum" (p. 481). On that note we turn to an examination of the predictive studies that have emphasized patterns of interaction and dyadic characteristics.

Dyadic Characteristics

Studies utilizing dyadic characteristics of courtship to predict later marital success fall into two broad types: retrospective and prospective. In retrospective studies couples are interviewed during their first year of marriage; this interview includes a structured assessment of characteristics of the premarital phase. The level of marital happiness is subsequently assessed several years into the marriage. The retrospective interview allows for detailed accounting of the process of relationship development over time. Prospective studies, on the other hand, use methods that assess couples premaritally and then follow couples through several years of marriage. These studies have the advantage of making predictions about the etiology of marital dysfunction.

Kelly, Huston, and Cate (1985) conducted retrospective interviews on courtship development with 50 newly married couples, followed by reinterviews of 21 of the couples 2 years later. These researchers assessed level of premarital love, conflict, maintenance, and ambivalence. Their results demonstrated that although premarital conflict was unrelated to premarital levels of love for the partner, premarital conflict was predictive of marital conflict and marital happiness 2.5 years later. Huston (in preparation), in a larger study involving a follow-up of 168 couples, replicated these previous findings. In addition, Huston found that greater ambivalence during courtship (particularly on the part of the female partner) and a slow, rocky movement to the stage of commitment predicted less satisfaction and stability of the marriage.

Surra, Arizzi and Asmussen (1988) conducted retrospective interviews with 41 newlywed couples and reinterviewed 39 of the couples 4 years later. Their interviews emphasized the reasons given for changes in commitment as the relationship progressed towards marriage; these reasons were subsequently coded into categories of intrapersonal-normative, dyadic, network influence and circumstantial. Dyadic reasons for commitment were positively related to marital happiness; specifically, couples who reported higher behavioral interdependence and self-disclosure as reasons for changes in commitment were happier 4 years later. Some intrapersonal-normative and network reasons were negatively related to marital happiness; couples reporting alternative partners, interaction with the social network, and comparison of the partner against a standard as reasons for changes in commitment also reported lower marital happiness 4 years later. Surra et al. (1988) discussed these findings in terms of "event-driven" versus "relationship-driven" courtships, the latter being viewed as leading to better mate choices.

Several of the prospective studies of dyadic characteristics involve behavioral observation of couples' communication patterns.

Markman (1979) assessed 14 premarital couples using the talk table. This device allows each partner to electronically record the positivity/negativity of the message sent to the other (intent) and of the message received from the other (impact). He assessed relationship satisfaction of the couples 1.0, 2.5, and 5.5 years later (Markman 1979, 1981, 1984). Dissatisfaction with the relationship at one year was unrelated to positivity or negativity of premarital communication. Contrary to the one-year findings, the findings for the 2.5-year and 5.5-year follow-ups were essentially identical; lower satisfaction was related to higher levels of negative premarital communication. These results fit very nicely with previous work (Huston, McHale, & Crouter, 1986), which demonstrated that the "honeymoon" phase may protect couples from the deleterious effects of negative communication patterns in the first year of marriage. After the first year, however, negative interaction appears to erode marital happiness.

Markman has expanded his original study of premarital communication patterns to several new samples of couples. One study (Julien, Markman, & Lindahl, 1989) examined 59 couples over time. Results indicated that higher levels of premarital positive escalation and lower levels of premarital negative escalation (escalation being defined as the probability that a particular behavior will be responded to by the partner with the same behavior) were predictive of higher marital satisfaction 4 years later. In an intervention-oriented study, Markman, Floyd, Stanley, and Storaasli (1988) developed a cognitive-behavioral marital distress prevention program. This program was completed by 21 couples; these couples were compared longitudinally to 21 control couples who received no intervention. At the 1.5-year follow-up, couples who had completed the program showed greater marital satisfaction than the control couples; at the 3-year follow-up, program couples reported greater marital satisfaction, greater sexual satisfaction and lower levels of problem intensity.

Filsinger and Thoma (1988) conducted a study very similar to Markman's original design (1979), although the coding of the observational data utilized a different scheme. These researchers assessed the communication patterns of 31 couples premaritally and then followed the couples for 5 years. They compared stable and unstable couples; results indicated that levels of premarital positive reciprocity characterized unstable couples at 1, 2, and 5 years. Premarital negative reciprocity differentiated unstable from stable couples at one year only. Relative to marital adjustment, premarital levels of positive and negative reciprocity did not predict later marital adjustment; however, the level of female interruption was negatively correlated with males' later adjustment. Filsinger and Thoma (1988) concluded that these results provided general support for the idea that communication patterns may precede later relationship stability and satisfaction.

O'Leary, Barling, Arias, Rosenbaum, Malone, and Tyree (1989) are engaged in a longitudinal study of a particular type of negative premarital interaction: physical aggression. They have followed 272 couples from one month premarriage to the third year of marriage. Couples who reported physical aggression at premarriage, 18 months of marriage and 30 months of marriage were significantly more dissatisfied with their marriages at 30 months than were couples reporting no aggression in their marriages. Furthermore, marital satisfaction for the aggressive group decreased over time (O'Leary et al., 1989).

Two other studies (Fowers & Olson, 1986; Larsen & Olson, 1988) have examined the predictive validity of the instrument PREPARE, a premarital assessment of 11 relationship areas: realistic expectations, personality issues, communication, conflict resolution, financial management, leisure activities, sexual relationship, children and marriage, family and friends, equalitarian roles, and religious orientation. This measure assesses both how positively couples view their relationships and the extent of their agreement on each area. In both studies premarital PREPARE scores significantly discriminated between satisfied and dissatisfied couples 2 to 3 years into marriage and between divorced and intact couples. These researchers (Fowers & Olson, 1986; Larsen & Olson, 1988) concluded that discord and dissatisfaction up to 3 years after marriage can be predicted from premarital characteristics.

❧ Conclusions

Certainly the events and processes of courtship "set the stage" for the quality and stability of marriage. Yet our interest in courtship is not fueled solely by its important implications for marriage. Courtship is inherently interesting on its own. As the stage of life wherein heterosexual love and romance first develop, courtship has engendered countless works of literature, poetry, song, and film. Throughout the centuries we have been enamored of many facets of the courtship experience from love at first sight to the "Romeo and Juliet effect." Courtship was one of the first topics addressed by family researchers; in the 1990s research on romantic relationships is exploding with new theories, methods, and findings.

In the following chapters we hope to present an organized view of what scholars have learned about courtship after more than 7 decades of research. First, it is important to explore the larger sociohistoric context of courtship. In Chapter 2 we examine the roots of modern courtship through an analysis of changes in customs of American courtship through the twentieth century. In Chapter 3 we examine the various theories and models of relationship development, including stage models of relationship development as well as interpersonal process models. Chapter 4 considers the intrapersonal, dyadic, network, and circumstantial factors (Surra, 1987) that influence courtship stability. Chapter 5 turns to a discussion of courtships in crisis, including the termination of courting relationships and the occurrence of physical violence and sexual aggression. Finally, in Chapter 6 we speculate on the factors that will shape courtship into the next century and discuss the future research needs in the field of courtship studies.

2

The History of Courtship

Courtship takes many forms, depending mainly on the point in history and the culture in which it exists. The choice of a mate in Europe several centuries ago was almost entirely determined by the families involved (Murstein, 1974), and this practice is currently observed in some present-day cultures. The current practice in most Western countries, however, is for potential partners to select mates on the basis of their personal preferences. Yet this free-choice situation should not imply that the mate-selection process is immune to such external influences as parents, friends, kin, social class, and circumstantial events. Although marital choice is determined by the participants, the relative importance of various decision factors has changed over time.[1]

‍❧ Courtship From Colonial Times to 1830

American courtship as it is known today owes its character to several antecedents stemming from Europe and characteristics embedded in the culture of the United States. Many factors in the "New World" worked to change the traditional courtship customs of European society. The weakening of kinship ties with European relatives as well as the migration of single individuals and nuclear families served to weaken parent-dominated marriages (Coontz, 1988; Tibbits, 1965). In fact, Tibbits' (1965) analysis of census data shows that the incidence of extended families in America was never large. Furthermore, the demands of life in the new frontier mitigated against long courtships and chaperones. The need for workers meant that the pioneer girl could not be "relegated to inertia" as her European sisters were; her labor was necessary to the continuation of the community (Murstein, 1976). In some communities the need for population was so great that bachelors were harassed, being fined for their singleness or run out of town. Marriage was clearly encouraged, and singleness was seen as a sign of sloth (Murstein, 1974).

Many scholars note that the American system of courtship contained elements of a participant-run system from its earliest days (Gadlin, 1977; Murstein, 1974; Rothman, 1984). Young people were granted autonomy in their choice of a mate. Parents exerted control largely through determining the timing of the marriage by withholding inheritance of land or the release of a son's labor (Glenn & Coleman, 1988; Greven, 1970; Rothman, 1984). The choice of a mate was based on reason; perhaps the single most important criterion for marriage readiness was the ability of the man to support a wife and family (Gadlin, 1977; Rothman, 1984). Other rational reasons for marriage were similar social standing and family approval of the prospective mate (Gadlin, 1977). Murstein (1976) argued that in the seventeenth and eighteenth centuries love was the natural expression of the spouse role (something that was to develop after marriage rather than before). Yet the emotional side of love was not entirely absent; for example, both the Puritans and the Quakers believed in the importance of affection to marital harmony (Coontz, 1988; Rothman, 1984). Several writers (Furstenberg, 1966; Rothman, 1984; Seward, 1978) noted that the roots of an intimate and affectionate courtship system were in place quite early in America. By the early 1800s the definition of love and affection no longer relied solely on "reason." According to Rothman (1984), love was supposed to be "more compelling than friendship, more lasting than passion, more serious than romance" (p. 36). Openness, candor, and sincerity were valued traits to look for in a potential mate; however, romantic love was not valued, for it was viewed as immature and unreliable (Rothman, 1984).

Young people spent nearly a decade choosing a marital partner (Rothman, 1984). They met in church, the neighborhood, and at home; few were strangers, for they had grown up together. The unchaperoned and intertwined lives of young men and women was strictly an American phenomenon as opposed to the relative segregation of the sexes in Europe (Demos, 1986; Murstein, 1974). Such integration made for a more relaxed style of interaction between men and women, a style that was often mistaken for coldness by Europeans (Murstein, 1974). Socializing, rather than being a "special" activity, was integrated into everyday life (Rothman, 1984). Young people in America interacted in mixed-sex groups; however couples could spend time alone walking, riding, or in the parlor (Murstein, 1974). Partners were relatively free to determine the nature of their premarital interactions (Furstenberg, 1966). Parents made little effort to oversee courtship; in fact, Rothman (1984) noted that parents would give a young couple privacy when a suitor came to call by going out for a walk or going to bed.

The autonomy of the courting couple is seen in the colonial practice of bundling. While bundling may never have been very widespread, as a courtship custom it has generated great interest (Rothman, 1984). Bundling consisted of a young woman inviting a suitor to go to bed with her, fully clothed, in some cases with a board placed between their bodies (Murstein, 1974; Stiles, 1871). Bundling was a privilege of the woman to bestow upon a favorite suitor (Rothman, 1984), and in situations where there was little room for privacy of the couple, bundling served as a time for the young people to get to know one another (Murstein, 1974). Bundling obviously must have taken place with the sanction of the young woman's parents.

Sexual passion, however, was to be contained (Rothman, 1984). Here again couples had great autonomy, for they were given the privacy necessary for the expression of physical affection. Rothman's analysis of late eighteenth century correspondence clearly shows the struggles of courting couples to contain their passions. She noted that couples did not always suppress their sexual desires; the premarital conception rate hit an all time high of 30% in the 1770s (Rothman, 1984). Premarital pregnancy was a sign of weakness rather than immorality; if the couple married, few sanctions were brought to bear (Coontz, 1988). Overall, the colonies were fairly open in their discussion of sexual matters (Coontz, 1988; Gadlin, 1977).

The views of sex outside of marriage and the sexuality of women began to change at the end of the eighteenth century. Earlier sexual freedom was replaced with an emphasis on self-control and chasteness (Coontz, 1988). The ministerial view of women as passionless gained momentum (Murstein, 1974); premarital pregnancy was now viewed as a sign of female impurity (Rothman, 1984). Yet the boundaries of sexual interaction were still loosely drawn; improper behavior of the man was likely to draw nothing more than a scolding, and flirting and sexual playfulness were still common (Rothman, 1984). Courting couples in the early nineteenth century responded to the dilemma of proper sexual restraint versus passion with the invention of petting, that is, sexual expression short of coitus (Rothman, 1984). In this way couples were able to maintain the sexual freedom of earlier times without fear of the consequences.

In the colonies and the early years of the republic there was not a sharp demarcation between home and commerce. This situation resulted in a relatively interdependent set of roles for men and women; labor was sex-typed but not rigidly divided into separate spheres (Coontz, 1988; Gadlin, 1977). Women enjoyed relatively greater participation in business and home manufacturing in the 1800s than in the next century, giving them a central role in the economy of the household (Margolis, 1984). Ironically, although viewed as "deputy husbands" and enjoying relatively more economic responsibility than nineteenth-century women, eighteenth-century women lacked a distinct sphere of influence (e.g., the home). The structure of male-female relationships was still largely patriarchal (Coontz, 1988).

Ultimately marriage represented different things for men and women. For men marriage meant the "end of aloneness" and the start of companionship; for women it meant a redefinition of the woman's existence and role in life. Marriage placed her in the unenviable position of bearing responsibility for the happiness of husband and children and yet being legally and financially dependent on her husband for her own well-being (Coontz, 1988; Rothman, 1984). Because she was also likely to be moving away from her support network of family and friends upon her marriage, young women of this time were none too eager to set a wedding date. A young woman may have employed delaying tactics to postpone the marriage to which her suitor so eagerly looked forward. A postwedding bridal trip often included friends and relatives in order to ease a woman's transition into the state of marriage (Rothman, 1984).

⪼ Courtship From 1830 to 1880

During the middle part of the nineteenth century the changing view of men and women was to have a pervasive effect on American courtship (Rothman, 1984). "Separate spheres" as an ideology emphasized the immutable differences between the sexes—from the mundane to the spiritual. A woman's nature was virtuous and angelic; she was capable of calming the wild nature of man (Coontz, 1988). In fact, she was his moral superior and was supposed to lead him to the path of virtue (Murstein, 1974). Her domesticity was prized; his ability to support his family was his most important goal. Rather than the interdependent relationship of husband and wife of rural colonial times (Gadlin, 1977), the mid-nineteenth century was marked by separation of the sexes. The cult of domesticity sanctified the home and gave women a revered place of their own (Coontz, 1988).

Despite an ideology of separate spheres for men and women, this was also a time of increasing equality for women. Women were gaining legal rights (e.g., the married women's property act of 1848) as well as increased earning power and education (Murstein, 1976). Young unmarried women worked in factories or did wage-producing activities at home; however, their role as wage earner was relinquished after marriage (Coontz, 1988; Demos, 1986). Women were actually viewed as morally superior to men, although this type of superiority was a double-edged sword, for because the woman held moral sway over the men of the household, it was felt that some legal rights (e.g., the vote) were unnecessary for her (Rothman, 1984). Thus social equality was not met with full legal or economic equality.

The separation of the spheres of men and women served to limit the ability of adolescent boys and girls to get to know one another (Rothman, 1984). Whereas before puberty boys and girls shared everyday life, after puberty young girls entered the "female world" and prepared for future housewifery (Demos, 1986). Once a courtship was begun, however, the couple was afforded a great deal of time together in private, without chaperones. Ultimately couples were still relatively autonomous in their choice of mate; often permission to marry was sought from the woman's parents only after the engagement was a foregone conclusion (Lystra, 1989).

Courtship became more formalized, as did life in general (Murstein, 1974), and the customs of formal announcement of the engagement and exchanging of engagement rings or other tokens of commitment began (Rothman, 1984). This was also the beginning of the formal wedding ceremony with a white dress and veil, symbolizing the purity of the bride.

Ironically, new expectations for candor and communication in marriage arose at the very time that men and women had less in common (Coontz, 1988). Despite the separation of the sexes (or perhaps because of the resulting idealization of women), romantic love began to flourish (Lystra, 1989). Romantic love, which had earlier been viewed as childish, was now viewed as the only acceptable basis for marriage (Coontz, 1988; Rothman, 1984). Romantic love contained elements of passion as well as mutuality, communion, sympathy, and candor (Rothman, 1984); romantic love was very emotionally intimate, and at the same time mysterious and unexplainable (Lystra, 1989). Romantic love centered around the concept of the "ideal self" (Lystra, 1989). The true inner person was to be revealed through extensive self disclosure and honesty with the loved one; thus romantic love embodied total self revelation and open communication.

Ultimately marriage based on romantic love was important to women, for it served to give them some assurance of long-term commitment. This was quite important because women during this era were nearly completely economically dependent upon their husbands. During courtship women often enacted a series of "secret tests" of their suitors' love in order to reassure themselves that the emotional bond was strong and worthy. Such tests might entail overcoming an obstacle (such as family disapproval, illness, religious differences, or a character flaw) or even the ultimate test of breaking off the engagement. Such tests also served to strengthen the emotional bond between the partners when the tests were successfully passed (Lystra, 1989).

Romantic love also entailed sexual passion and expression (Lystra, 1989). Because standards for premarital sexual behavior were tightening, however, sexual intercourse was clearly reserved for marriage (Rothman, 1984). The range of acceptable sexual behavior had become more constrained over the nineteenth century, so that, publicly at least, petting became unacceptable behavior (Coontz, 1988). Although women were supposed to be passionless, or at the very least in control of the passion of their suitors, both Lystra's (1989) and Rothman's (1984) analyses demonstrated that affectionate behavior still occurred in courtship. Rothman (1984) offers one example in which "kisses" were something to be "stolen" by a suitor and "doled out" as a reward by his loved one (p. 126). Young women were given the responsibility to control affectional expression in courtship; Rothman (1984) clearly demonstrates that not only did a young woman have to control her suitor's ardor, but often she had to control her own passion as well. Thus the ministerial view of women as passionless was not always totally embraced by women themselves. Despite the public condemnation of sexual expression, privately courting couples expressed sexual enthusiasm and openness (Lystra, 1989).

The link between marriage and the establishment of a home was strong (Rothman, 1984). A man's readiness for marriage was still gauged by his ability to provide a home for his new wife; however, in the face of rising standards of middle-class affluence, such provision became more difficult over time (Rothman, 1984). Owning a home was not always possible, and as an alternative, one half to two thirds of urban newlyweds boarded with strangers rather than living with the family of origin (Coontz, 1988). The young woman was responsible for the interior furnishings of the home, and she often saved her wages for this purpose. Wedding gifts became increasingly common, especially as a sign of conspicuous consumption (Rothman, 1984).

৯ Courtship From 1880 to 1920

The theme of separate spheres persisted through the late nineteenth century but with an added twist. Now, rather than being possessed of wild spirits, men were viewed as depraved; their immorality became a grave social problem (Rothman, 1984). Men had to learn to control their animal passions; this could only be accomplished through women's modesty. Yet, although modest and moral, women were also seen as needing protection due to their physical and intellectual inferiority (Smith-Rosenberg, 1985).

The separate spheres of men and women widened further. Although youth spent more time with the opposite sex in school and work, the lives of young women and young men rarely intersected due to separate spheres in school curricula (Rothman, 1984). The ideology of separate spheres permeated the world of work as well; men and women did not compete for the same jobs (Margolis, 1984). When young men and women were together, the propriety of the times demanded that males and females keep their distance; the purity of the young woman had to be guarded. In the upper classes chaperones became a common fixture (Rothman, 1984).

Romantic love became ever more romantic. Love was supposed to be effortless, a strong magnet pulling the couple together (Rothman, 1984). Women were believed to love less intensely than men; in courtship men placed more emphasis on their feelings than did women, most likely a result of men's greater control over their own futures (Rothman, 1984). Separate spheres also resulted in the increasing importance of same-sex friends to young married women (Coontz, 1988; Smith-Rosenberg, 1985).

The customs of courtship had become increasingly formal. After a young woman had her first "season," she was eligible to receive callers (Bailey, 1988). A young man and young woman had to be formally introduced before they were allowed to speak to one another (Waller, 1951). After such an introduction, the young woman's mother would ask the young man to call upon her daughter; later on the young lady could do the asking (Bailey, 1988). In the early stages of courtship long rides and late hours were frowned upon; most courting activities took place in the girl's home (Waller, 1951). There was an elaborate system of etiquette designed to let the young man know whether he was welcome to call again in the future. After an engagement the couple was given more privacy and time alone; however, chastity was still valued. If the relationship lasted too long or became too intimate, it was supposed to result in an engagement (Bailey, 1988). In fact, calling upon a young lady was eventually supposed to end in only one goal—marriage.

The elaborate system of calling was not feasible for the less wealthy, however. Families living in one or two rooms did not have the space available for courtship in the home; so working-class youth courted in public (Bailey, 1988). In addition, increasing urbanization meant that many young people were on their own, working in the cities (Coontz, 1988). Because rules of propriety dictated that a young woman could not have a gentleman in her apartment, boardinghouse or dorm room, courtship activities had to take place in the public domain. Eventually the wealthy saw the less formal system of courtship in public as something to emulate, and the fun and excitement of "dating" became an upper-class phenomenon as well (Bailey, 1988; Coontz, 1988).

"Going somewhere" became the activity of courtship and the pastime of youth by the turn of the century (Rothman, 1984). In earlier times young people had gone alone to dances or stayed out late without adult supervision; however, these activities took place within a system of informal community control (Koller, 1951). Now that system of informal controls was loosening as courtship moved into the dance halls and cabarets (Bailey, 1988). Ironically, the movement of courtship from the home to the public sphere afforded less privacy and time to get to know one another. While the cabaret allowed for more sexual experimentation, it did not allow for emotional openness and candor (Rothman, 1984).

At the turn of the century it was still up to the woman to keep sexual behavior in check (Rothman, 1984). Sexual restraint was important, and the ideology of woman as sexless still held sway (Coontz, 1988). Yet liberal norms of sexual behavior were developing in some segments of society (e.g., Bohemian culture), and by 1910 these norms had begun to spread to the rest of the country. The link between sex and marriage was still strong, and sexual fulfillment was seen as an important component of a happy marriage. This ideology eventually led to an emphasis on sexual experimentation before marriage, and the rate of premarital intercourse for women increased sharply. While 87% of women born before 1890 were virgins at marriage, only 30% of those born after 1910 "waited until marriage." The comparable figures for men were 49% and 14% virgins at marriage for the pre-1890 and post-1910 birth cohorts (Terman, 1938).[2] A virtuous woman, however, still only had sex with the man that she was about to marry.

↜ Courtship From 1920 to 1945

By 1920 the centerpiece of twentieth-century American courtship was firmly in place—dating. Dating involved informal, unchaperoned, male-female interaction with no specific commitment (Murstein, 1974). The rules of dating were established by the peer group rather than the community at large (Modell, 1983). Bailey (1988) attributed the rise of dating in the first part of the twentieth century to both the creation of adolescence as a distinct period of the life cycle and to the emergence of mass culture. The former trend created an atmosphere wherein the selection of a mate could be delayed, and the latter trend provided a uniform set of rules of etiquette to be followed by all. Other scholars cite the shift from rural to urban society, the emancipation of women, the emphasis on companionate marriage, widespread ownership of cars, the emergence of motion pictures, and the resulting decrease in community control as forces which brought dating into being (Burgess & Wallin, 1954; Lynd & Lynd, 1929; Murstein, 1974). Dating was to quickly become the major recreational pastime of youth (Waller, 1951).

Dating entailed something that was entirely new in the courtship system—the need for money (Bailey, 1988; Lynd & Lynd, 1929). Dating meant "going out" to do things rather than visiting in the young woman's home, and going out in public required money. Although courtship had always had an economic basis (e.g., a man's readiness to marry was contingent on his ability to support a family, and a poor man could not call on a rich female), dating made a man's access to a woman contingent on money in a very direct way. Dating also changed the balance of power in the courting relationship. When courtship was centered in the home, the woman was more in control, but as courtship shifted to the public sphere and the need for money arose, control also shifted to the man (Bailey, 1988).

Perhaps the best example of this economic basis of courtship comes from Waller's (1937) classic study of the "rating and dating" complex on the Penn State campus. By the time of Waller's study, dating as a courtship activity was no longer about "love"; rather, it was about competition (Bailey, 1988). The trend toward conspicuous consumption during the 1800s (Rothman, 1984) reached its culmination in the era of rating and dating (Bailey, 1988). The men who rated were those who could afford a car, fancy dinners, flowers, and the best seats at the theater; the women who were sought after were those who were rated as popular by virtue of their ability to date different men three to four times a week (Waller, 1937). Women also "rated" through their ability to adhere to the current standards of beauty held up by popular culture (Bailey, 1988).

Lynd and Lynd (1929) alluded to the presence of a "rating and dating" ideology even in the high schools of Middletown; popular girls went to the best dances, wore expensive clothes, and belonged to the "right" clubs. Indeed, the extracurricular events of the high schools provided the infrastructure for the entire system of dating (Modell, 1983). Although some scholars have questioned whether "rating and dating" was as widespread as Waller implied (see Gordon, 1981; Murstein, 1974; Rothman, 1984), it remains an interesting example of the emphasis on consumption rather than love. Both Bailey (1988) and Coontz (1988) noted that marriage came to be discussed in economic terms at this time as well.

The most popular pastimes on dates were dancing and going to the movies (Lynd & Lynd, 1929, 1937; Rothman, 1984). Whereas before the turn of the century a dance was a group activity, in the 1920s dancing was couple oriented. Dancing allowed a young man and woman the excitement of physical closeness without the dangers of sex (Modell, 1983; Rothman, 1984). Another powerful influence on dating was the automobile; the car allowed a great deal of privacy and intimacy, and the practice of petting spread (Lynd & Lynd, 1937). Both Lynd and Lynd (1929) and Rothman (1984) remarked that "petting parties" became a regular occurrence in the high schools of the 1920s.

It should be noted that the system of dating was somewhat independent of the system of courting for marriage (Rothman, 1984). This two-tiered system of heterosexual interaction stands in sharp contrast to the courtship system of the eighteenth and nineteenth centuries. In the twentieth century dating was a vehicle for getting to know someone before settling into an exclusive pairing (Burgess & Wallin, 1954). Dating and courtship had different objectives. Dating focused on success and increasing one's popularity without becoming emotionally involved, whereas courtship focused on finding a mate who exhibited the traits of emotional maturity, honesty, genuineness, and a desire for family life (Waller, 1951). Dating left off and courtship began once a young woman and a young man began keeping "steady company." A graduated series of dates was considered the first step into a serious romance (Modell, 1983). By the 1930s "steady" relationships had developed as a stage between the casualness of dating and the commitment to marry (Gordon, 1981; Modell, 1983).

Portions of the nineteenth-century conception of male and female sexuality continued into the twentieth century; men were presumed to be interested in sex, and women were expected to control sex in the relationship by saying "no" (Bailey, 1988). Sexual expression was liberalizing, however. The culture of adolescence brought with it new norms of liberal sexual behavior (Bailey, 1988), and relations between the sexes were characterized by greater frankness (Lynd & Lynd, 1929). Caplow, Bahr, Chadwick, Hill, and Williamson (1982) remarked that the 1920s represented a period of sexual and social revolution unmatched until the late 1960s: sex was the dominant theme of movies and literature, the code of behavior for women liberalized (e.g., women initiated dates), the incidence of premarital intercourse was on the rise, and legal rights for women took hold.

Despite liberalization, a double standard of sexual behavior blamed women for sexual transgressions (even rape) (Bailey, 1988). Unless she was truly pure, she was considered cheap and fair game; the good-girl versus bad-girl dichotomy abounded (Modell, 1983). Such a depiction of the sexual natures of men and women failed to recognize the increasing pressure placed on women to repay the debt engendered by a man's spending money on a date (Bailey, 1988). Despite the pressure, most of the women who had premarital sex had intercourse only with the man they were engaged to marry. As noted above, the rate of change in the incidence of premarital intercourse was most remarkable from pre- to post-1900; from the 1920s to the 1960s the incidence of premarital intercourse was fairly stable, ranging from 50% to 85% for men and from 30% to 65% for women (Caplow et al., 1982). While virginity was still desirable in a bride, it was no longer a requirement (Rothman, 1984).

Romantic love was considered the only basis of marriage, and evidence of the romantic ideal is apparent in Lynd and Lynd's (1929) discussion of marriage in Middletown. Mate selection was based on "mysterious attraction" and was supposed to happen almost by chance. Youth were taught that they would know it when they found the "right one." There was an increasing emphasis on the couple relationship and higher expectations for emotional closeness (Coontz, 1988). The continuation of romanticism, however, seems curiously absent in the Lynds' description of the relatively separate lives of husbands and wives. Sex roles in the 1920s and 1930s were clearly still organized around separate spheres for men and women (Lynd & Lynd, 1929, 1937). The roots of equality for women were firmly in place, however, as enfranchisement, legal rights, and greater freedom in divorce developed during the first three decades of the twentieth century (Kelley, 1969).[3]

The rating and dating scene was disrupted by the Great Depression and the Second World War. College enrollments declined as did the influence of fraternities, and women entered the labor force with a vengeance (Margolis, 1984; Rothman, 1984). Courtship activities were literally put on hold for college-age youth (Bailey, 1988), although younger adolescents continued on with the social patterns of the 1930s (Lynd & Lynd, 1937; Rothman, 1984). An early inkling of the 1950s urge for stability in family relationships may be seen in the rise in "secret" high school marriages noted by the Lynds in

Middletown during the Depression (Lynd & Lynd, 1937). The changes in the world at large were to have a profound impact on the courtship system after World War II.

❧ Courtship From 1945 to 1960

One of the most notable demographic trends of the twentieth century is the drop in the age at first marriage and the increase in the marriage rate during the late 1940s and early 1950s. By 1950 the age at marriage was at its lowest point for the twentieth century: 22 years for men and 20 years for women (Mintz & Kellogg, 1988). Whether fueled by a desire for stability after years of upheaval, the much publicized "man shortage," or a desire of youth to assert their independence (Bailey, 1988; Modell, 1989), the increasingly younger age at marriage had important effects on courtship and dating. Dating activities were starting at an earlier age; by junior high school group dating was common, with a group of boys meeting up with a group of girls and subsequently pairing off (Rothman, 1984). These youth began dating in earnest in high school (more than three quarters of youth reported dating during high school, Burgess & Wallin, 1953), with "going steady" as the new centerpiece of the dating system (Kelley, 1969). Going steady brought a whole new set of rituals, including tokens of commitment (such as a class ring), a specified number of telephone calls and dates each week, and the implication of greater sexual intimacy (Bailey, 1988). Although youth were likely to go steady several times by the end of high school (Rothman, 1984), going steady often entailed strong affection and love for the partner (Burgess & Wallin, 1953). Burgess and Wallin (1953) rejected the notion of "dating as dalliance" for this generation and reported that the majority of steady relationships were relatively long in duration.

Popularity for girls now rested on their ability to attract a "steady." Unfortunately, such popularity often meant early marriage and low educational attainment for women (Modell, 1989). Those youth who did not go on to college married soon after graduation (Rothman, 1984), after a courtship of 1 to 2 years in length (Burgess & Wallin, 1953). For college women, "landing a man" by senior year was an openly acknowledged goal (Bailey, 1988).

Parental reaction to going steady was not positive, especially as parents feared a resulting increase in premarital sexual behavior (Bailey, 1988). Simultaneously, the emphasis on early marriage was seen as a "moral" way of dealing with the issue of youth sexuality (Bailey, 1988). The "good girl" engaged in every form of petting except intercourse—or at least that's all she admitted to with her peer group (Rubin, 1976). The incidence of premarital intercourse for both men and women, however, was still about the same as it had been during the 1920s (Caplow et al., 1982). Burgess and Wallin (1953) reported premarital intercourse rates of 67% for men and 46% for women. Ehrmann's (1959) study of premarital sexuality demonstrated similar rates for males only: 62% for men and 15% for women. The difference in rates for females reflects the different samples utilized; Burgess and Wallin (1953) studied engaged couples, whereas Ehrmann studied college students in general. A woman still was most likely to engage in intercourse only with the man she intended to marry. Indeed the likelihood of intercourse occurring during an engagement was directly proportional to the length of that engagement (Burgess & Wallin, 1953).

Love was still the primary basis for marriage. Marriage was seen as the most important source of happiness and fulfillment; single men and women were to be pitied because they could not achieve a state of happiness without a spouse (Mintz & Kellogg, 1988; Stein, 1976). Couples emphasized compatibility and common interests as well as love as reasons for the selection of their mates (Burgess & Wallin, 1953). The companionate marriage with complementary roles of provider and homemaker was the ideal to be strived for (Mintz & Kellogg, 1988).

The emphasis on masculinity and femininity also changed during the postwar period. Advances in the understanding of prenatal development helped foster the idea that gender identity was a fragile entity (Bailey, 1988). Coupled with this was a fear that the "provider role" of men was being undermined by the wartime influx of women into industry (Margolis, 1984). This fear resulted in a postwar campaign to help men rediscover their masculinity—largely through an emphasis on increased femininity in women and a return of the cult of domesticity (Bailey, 1988).[4] The formula for marital bliss was a

return to the passive female (Lundberg & Farnham, 1947). In courtship this meant that women had to demonstrate their frailties—their
need to be protected and their inferior mental capacity. The new etiquette of courtship further reinforced a man's right to be dominant
and made female submissiveness a requirement in a date (Bailey,
1988). The vision of the perfect relationship included sacrificing for
the other, avoidance of conflict, and a great deal of togetherness
(Kidd, 1975).

❧ Courtship From 1960 to the Present

All was not well in the idealized family of the 1950s. Betty Friedan
(1963) identified it as the "problem that has no name"; later it would
come to be known as the "woman thing" (Cohen, 1988). Discontent
with the restricted role of wife and mother led many young women
to first question the role that marriage would play in their lives and
later to postpone marriage in favor of educational and career pur-
suits (Mintz & Kellogg, 1988). As the women's movement progressed,
marriage and childbearing were increasingly couched in terms of
oppression and exploitation of women (Cohen, 1988). The feminist
emphasis on a reexamination of marriage and gender was to affect
profoundly the ways in which both men and women approached
courtship.

Simultaneously, the resurgence of youth culture and the generation gap encouraged young people to define themselves in a manner
distinct from that of their parents (Mintz & Kellogg, 1988). This
youth culture was associated with an increasingly liberal attitude
toward premarital sexual behavior; however, the revolution in sexual attitudes and behavior extended far beyond adolescents, as reflected in changes in fashion, media, and movies (Mintz & Kellogg,
1988). Changes in attitudes toward nonmarital sex were similarly
affected by the increased availability of birth control and the extension of youth. Youth as a life stage was extended in both directions;
the increasing emphasis on educational attainment extended the
upper bound of youth (Mintz & Kellogg, 1988), whereas the decreasing age of menarche and sexual maturation across the twentieth
century extended the lower bound of youth (McCary, 1973). As a

result, young people spent more of their sexually mature lives outside of marriage (Mintz & Kellogg, 1988).

Significant changes in the incidence of premarital intercourse, especially for women, occurred during this period. By 1980 upwards of 80% of male and 65% of female college freshmen reported premarital sexual experience (Robinson & Jedlicka, 1982). Moreover, the timing of intercourse changed; whereas in the 1950s women were likely to have premarital sex during engagement, by the 1970s they were more likely to engage in sexual intercourse while going steady (Ehrmann, 1959; Wolfe, 1981). Youth were engaging in intercourse at earlier ages; Zelnick and Kanter (1980) found the average age at first intercourse to be 16 for males and 17 for females. Heated media attention to the contrary, sexuality among youth was not promiscuous, but, rather, was limited to a few partners (Caplow et al., 1982).

The increased equality of women had pervasive effects upon many aspects of courtship. Between 1960 and 1972 the proportion of women attending college increased threefold (Glick, 1975); by the early 1980s the number of women in college equaled the number of men for the first time. The trend of greater college attendance for both men and women through the 1970s and the increased emphasis on careers for women encouraged the delay of the age at first marriage. By 1988 the age at first marriage was 25.9 years for men and 23.6 years for women, the highest it had been since the turn of the century (Surra, 1990).

Some of the courtship patterns of the 1950s persisted into the 1970s and 1980s but with a few new twists. Dating and going steady were still central features of the courtship system; however, adolescents of the 1970s did not date as often and they began to date at an older age than they had in the 1950s (average age for females of 13 in 1958 and 14 in 1978). The first experience with going steady, however, was occurring at slightly younger ages, dropping from age 17 in 1958 to age 16 in 1978 (Bell & Coughey, 1980). Rice (1990) noted that dating in the 1970s and 1980s changed in three important ways: there was greater opportunity for informal opposite-sex interaction, dating became less formal than in previous generations, and there was no longer a set progression of stages from first meeting to marriage. In other words, the dating system became more pluralistic over time. For example, it became increasingly acceptable for women to initiate dating activities and to be responsible for the economics of the date (Modell, 1983). While not equalitarian, dating (and marriage) were nevertheless moving away from a strictly patriarchal ideology.

Changes in sexual behavior and delay of marriage were accompanied by a new stage in the courtship system: cohabitation. Although cohabitation was first studied as a life-style of college youth (e.g., Macklin, 1972), recent studies demonstrate that 40% to 50% of all youth cohabit at some point before age 30 (Surra, 1990). There is speculation that cohabitation will emerge in the future as a relatively common stage of relationship development. Interestingly, at the same time there has been a seemingly contradictory trend toward more "older" youth (ages 18-35) living at home with their parents (Coontz, 1988).

The 1950s vision of the perfect relationship had changed by the late 1960s. Now the emphasis was on totally open communication, self-fulfillment, creative and unique forms of interaction, and relationships as inherently changeable (Kidd, 1975). This vision persisted until the late 1970s (Prusank, Duran, & DeLillo, 1991).

Thus the 1960s and 1970s were characterized by a profound shift in values and behavior. Ironically, while the new values emphasized self-fulfillment, they simultaneously focused on marriage as a source of intense emotional intimacy and companionship (Mintz & Kellogg, 1988). Farber's (1964) "permanent available" model highlights the end product of this dual emphasis on individuality and intimacy. Farber argued that marriage did not necessarily take one out of the courtship system because increasingly easy access to divorce made the matter of changing partners relatively simple. Ultimately, however, courting couples still married for the same reasons their parents did: love and emotional commitment. In fact, states Coontz (1988), over time the importance of love in mate selection increased to such a degree that "the degree of emotional satisfaction . . . demanded from husband-wife . . . relations in the twentieth century would have astounded previous generations" (p. 356).

In the last decade there have been inklings of a return to a more conservative system of courtship. While the women's movement emphasized the alternatives available to women, the ideology of the importance of having a mate for women has not diminished a great deal. A perusal of the popular literature for women reveals a strong emphasis on "finding and keeping a man," often through the traditional wiles of femininity. In the early 1980s the "man shortage" created a nationwide furor (see Salholz, Michael, Starr, Doherty, Abramson, & Wingert, 1986), and sent the message that women could have education or marriage but not both. The vision of the perfect relationship now emphasized the importance of balancing togetherness and individuality, other-orientation and self-fulfillment, and communicating openly while protecting the partner's feelings (Prusank et al., 1991). Concern over sexually transmitted diseases such as AIDS has caused a harkening back to monogamous sexual relationships (Megli & Morgan, 1991; Mintz & Kellogg, 1988). The 1980s saw the resurgence of formal dances and proms as well as an increase in elaborate and formal weddings, and tradition was in (Bailey, 1988). Whether these trends signal a return to conservatism in courtship and marriage remains to be seen in the ensuing decades.

‌ Conclusions

Throughout the history of courtship in America there are themes of both continuity and change. Change occurred in many ways. Control over the activities of courtship went from female to male to semiequalitarian; the places of courtship changed "from front porch to backseat" (the title of Beth Bailey's 1988 book), courtship increasingly required access to monetary resources, and the nature of sexual activity cycled through periods of openness versus inhibition. The gatekeepers of courtship also changed from informal community control to parental oversight to the participants themselves.

There are nevertheless several themes of continuity. American youth have always enjoyed relative autonomy in choosing their mates; and, surprisingly, the number of partners seriously considered for marriage seems to have remained relatively constant. Koller (1951) found little change in the number of men regarded as serious possibilities for mates in his study of three generations of Ohio women.

Most of the women, whether keeping company in the 1890s or going steady in the 1950s, seriously considered only one man—their future husbands! Burgess and Wallin (1953) reported that 30% of their engaged couples had been involved in no serious romance other than the present one; the majority of the couples reported only one or two serious relationships in their lives. Robins and Huston's (1983) assessment of compatibility testing in the 1980s is striking in its similarity. They found that men and women had on average only two other serious relationships before meeting their future husbands and wives. What is it about courtship that almost literally translates one's readiness to marry into a decision to marry the next partner with whom one becomes seriously involved? In the remainder of this volume we will explore this question.

☙ Notes

1. The history of courtship is limited largely to the history of white, middle-class and upper-class courting customs (Rothman, 1984). Information on courtship patterns among ethnic families (particularly black families under slavery), working-class families, and poor families is rather sketchy, and unfortunately has limited our ability to review courtship for these groups in the present volume.

2. Caplow et al. (1982) remark that Terman's figures are higher than those of Kinsey and other authors.

3. This emancipation, however, did not include "freedom to pursue a career." From 1920 to 1930 there was only a one percent rise in female employment (Margolis, 1984).

4. This cult of domesticity was in sharp contrast to the influx of women into the labor force during the Depression and World War II. The postwar campaign to get women out of the labor force was not entirely successful, however. By 1950, 24% of married women and 22% of women with children were working for wages. By 1960 nearly 39% of mothers with school-aged children were working full or part time (Margolis, 1984). These figures presage the later rapid influx of women into the labor force in the late 1960s and early 1970s. During the 1950s, however, there was still no doubt that for the working woman, marriage and family were the source of personal fulfillment.

3

Stage and Interpersonal Process Models of Courtship

In Chapter 2 we have shown that mate selection over the last few hundred years in the United States has predominately been a matter of individual choice, although at different points in time parental approval has been important. Ultimately, the American courtship system has been controlled by the partners involved. Consequently, mate selection theories during this century have focused on factors that operate in this "open market" system of mate choice. In the present chapter we trace the development of these major models.

As might be expected, the early scientific attempts at uncovering the important factors involved in courtship relied on prevailing theories of individual behavior, mainly Freudian psychology with its heavy emphasis on unconscious processes (Murstein, 1976). By and large these efforts were not fruitful. For example, Hamilton and

MacGowan (1929) found that only a small number of males and females reported marrying someone who resembled their opposite-sex parent, an hypothesis derived from the Oedipal complex. In response to such negative findings, models began to be developed that assumed conscious, rational choice by potential mates. The first of these to be discussed are rather static models that posit a single process as dominant during mate selection, for example, need complementarity (Winch, 1955a) and similarity (Burgess & Wallin, 1953) models. Later models suggested that different mate selection factors operated in a sequential fashion over time in a relationship. These models were substantially challenged on empirical and conceptual grounds but did suggest areas for further exploration. Finally, we present the most recently developed model, the interpersonal process model, which assumes that mate choice is a complex phenomenon and likely results from multiple factors at different levels of analysis.

ᴥ Antecedents of the Stage Models

The earliest models of courtship assumed that a single dimension of relationships, for example, need complementarity (Winch, 1955a) or attitude similarity (Burgess & Wallin, 1953) operated over the length of the premarital relationship to influence the choice of a potential marital partner. In other words, the assumption was that individuals looked for a future marital partner on the basis of one overriding dimension that was sufficient to convince the chooser to stay with that partner until the marriage day. These early models have been referred to as "compatibility models" (e.g., Cate & Lloyd, 1988; Levinger & Rands, 1985). The term "compatibility" in these earlier models implied that marital choice was determined by individuals in courtships examining the extent to which their various stable psychological or demographic attributes matched (e.g., complemented or were similar to) those of their partners. A match signified that partners were compatible with each other and would thus be propelled to marriage.

Complementary Needs

One of the earliest formal compatibility models of mate selection is a more complex version of the layperson's postulate that "opposites attract." Winch's (1955a) complementary needs theory assumed that individuals have certain psychological needs and that people seek marital partners who can fulfill or "complement" those needs. Supposedly, compatibility is induced by Partner B either enacting behaviors that satisfy a need in Partner A, or Partner B avoiding certain behaviors that would conflict with Partner A. In other words, complementarity can exist when one partner has a high need in one personality area with the other partner having a low need in that same area (e.g., one partner having a high need for submissiveness and the other having a low need for submissiveness). On the other hand, complementarity can exist when different needs are gratified within the couple (e.g., one partner having a need to be dominant and the other having a need to be submissive). Winch (Winch, 1955b; Winch, Ktsanes, & Ktsanes, 1954) reported support for this theory through the results of two studies that used psychoanalytic assessments of needs interviews as well as the answers of interviewees to projective testing. Unfortunately, although the idea of "complementary needs" has great appeal in folk wisdom, there was a lack of empirical support for the theory. The findings of Winch's studies have received serious criticism on the basis of faulty conceptualization and interpretation as well as a lack of replication (see Murstein, 1976; Seyfried, 1977; and Tharp, 1963, for comprehensive critiques of the theory).

Similarity

In contrast to the complementarity model, the similarity model holds that mate selection operates according to the lay hypothesis that "birds of a feather flock together." In other words, the theory holds that individuals select marital partners on the basis of whether they are similar to each other on an array of attributes. Empirical evidence appears to support this model in that both premarital and marital partners have been found to be similar in attitudes and values (Burgess & Wallin, 1953; Schellenberg, 1960), personality (Antill, 1983), physical attractiveness (Price & Vandenberg, 1979), and several demographic characteristics such as age, religion, race, ethnicity, etc. (Hendrick, 1981; Hill, Rubin, & Peplau, 1976). Similarity might produce compatibility through several processes: (a) direct reinforcement, (b) confirmation of people's sense of esteem or worth, (c) the implication that the partner may provide rewards in the future, and so on (Huston & Levinger, 1978). As with complementarity models, similarity models have received criticism. The fact that individuals tend to interact with people living close to them and also are likely to be socially similar limits opportunity to select others who are not similar to themselves, thus shedding doubt on whether similarity plays a direct role in the actual decision-making process (Kerckhoff, 1974). In other words, because we live near and are likely to interact with those who are already very similar (in terms of race, education, age, etc.), our chances of meeting a similar other are heightened by mere proximity rather than systematic choice. In addition, some empirical evidence suggests that the observed similarity in values and world views of couples evolves over time through their interaction together, rather than being used as an initial selection factor (Stephen, 1985). Other empirical evidence shows that similarity does not distinguish between couples who break up and those who stay together (Hill et al., 1976). Last, recent research shows that individuals who seriously dated several people before marriage (i.e., those with a higher probability of meeting a compatible mate) are found to be no more compatible than those who seriously dated only a few people (Robins, 1985).

❧ Stage Models of Courtship

Stage models of courtship portray the selection of a mate as proceeding through a sequential series of stages, with each stage focusing on certain processes in decision-making concerning a possible marriage mate. The development of these more complex models likely reflected the realization by researchers that interpersonal behavior in mate selection could not be explained with such simple models as similarity and complementarity. In the remainder of this chapter we discuss four stage models of courtship:

1. Reiss's Wheel theory (1960, 1980)
2. Kerckhoff and Davis's Filter theory (1962)
3. Murstein's Stimulus-Value-Role model (1970, 1976, 1987)
4. Lewis's Premarital Dyadic Formation framework (1972, 1973a)

Reiss's Wheel Theory

The Wheel theory of love (Reiss, 1960, 1980) was one of the earliest attempts to specify a developmental model of courtship that specified stages. This model was developed in response to the lack of attention by theoreticians to background factors that likely influence courtship decisions. This model posits that there are four stages or processes that people go through in developing a love relationship that will move toward marriage, although couples can cycle through the processes multiple times:

1. rapport
2. self-revelation
3. mutual dependency
4. intimacy need fulfillment

According to this model the first sequential process is that of developing *rapport* (e.g., feeling at ease, able to communicate and to "understand") between partners. This rapport facilitates communication, which increases the chance that the relationship will develop further. Rapport supposedly develops out of partners' assessments of the similarity of their backgrounds and attitudes.

Once rapport is established, the model proposes that partners can then engage more freely in *self-revelation* (e.g., revealing one's values, political beliefs, religious beliefs, etc.). Self-revelation, however, is influenced by broader sociological phenomena (social class, religion, etc.), such that the extent of disclosure that is desirable will vary. In the middle class it may be desirable to reveal quite intimate matters, whereas individuals from blue- collar backgrounds may desire less disclosure (Rubin, 1976).

This model proposes that the act of revealing the self on the part of both partners builds a feeling of *mutual dependency* or interdependency. In other words, both partners begin to rely on each other to obtain certain rewards that are not as readily or satisfactorily available from other partners; partners begin to take on unique significance for each other. Again, cultural and background factors likely influence the nature of the rewards on which people become dependent.

The last stage of this model proposes that individuals who have successfully passed through the previous stages will begin to assess whether their relationships provide *intimacy need fulfillment.* These needs are those that relate to the development of closeness between pairs, such as a need for someone to disclose to or to love. These needs are also seen as being sensitive to cultural and social influences, especially those that relate to social roles in the family.

Kerckhoff and Davis's Filter Theory

This theory or model is an outgrowth of the attention given to the compatibility models of similarity and complementarity discussed earlier. The Kerckhoff and Davis (1962) study was unique because it was designed to test the ability of similarity and complementarity to explain premarital selection processes over time with a sample of dating couples. Most previous studies had examined possible mate-selection factors in couples who were already married or premarital couples at only one point in time. Such studies could yield little information about the causal factors involved in mate selection.

This filter model was based on research that followed dating couples over an 8-month period, thus potentially allowing the researchers to make more valid inferences about the factors involved in selecting a marital partner. Women in college classes who were at least seriously attached to a premarital partner were recruited to fill out questionnaires and were asked to supply the name of their male partners. The males were then mailed identical questionnaires and asked to return them. This initial questionnaire asked the participants to fill out instruments that assessed their degree of value consensus and need complementarity. Eight months later both partners were sent a shorter questionnaire that asked them to indicate whether they were closer to being a permanent couple since they were first contacted, farther from being a permanent couple, or the same as when first asked.

The findings of this study showed that for the entire group only value consensus was related to progress toward marriage over the 8-month period. The predictors of courtship progress differed, however, according to how long couples had been dating each other. For couples who had been dating each other fewer than 18 months, only value consensus predicted progress toward marriage. On the other hand, for those dating longer than 18 months, only need complementarity predicted courtship progress. Interestingly, the relationship of similarity on various background factors (e.g., education, fathers' occupation, and religion) to courtship progress was not significant for either short-term or long-term couples. This finding suggested that people had already selected partners on the basis of these social characteristics prior to the study.

The findings from this study led to the development of a mate-selection model based on a proposed sequence of filters. The model posits that the first factor on which people filter or narrow down prospective mates is that of *social characteristics*, such as religion, education, etc. The second sequential factor on which people evaluate potential partners is *similarity* in attitudes and values. Once potential partners are narrowed down on the basis of these two filters, the degree of *need complementarity* is the final factor on which partners are selected.

Murstein's Stimulus-Value-Role Model

The original filter model discussed above was elaborated by Murstein (1970, 1976, 1987) in his presentation of the Stimulus-Value-Role model (SVR). This model assumes that the process of mate selection differs somewhat depending on whether partners exist in an "open" or "closed" field situation. Open situations are those that allow considerable freedom by the individual to initiate interactions with others (a party, brief encounters in day-to-day living, etc.), whereas closed situations are those that tend to induce interaction due to the roles that people play in certain situations (boss-employee interactions, committee chair-committee member interactions, etc.). The nature of these roles is assumed to be determined by society, interaction with parents, past interpersonal interaction, or genetic predispositions. The theory was developed from three studies, two of which were longitudinal in nature and one that was cross-sectional; however, many of the findings in support of the theory are cross-sectional.

The first stage of this SVR theory posits that in an open field setting people will consider as partners those who have certain *stimulus* characteristics, given that the pool of eligibles is already somewhat contextually restricted to others who are socially similar. Particular emphasis is placed on the stimulus of physical attractiveness as a selection factor in an open field setting and the likelihood that attraction will be reciprocal. Much research has shown the potency of physical attractiveness in predicting who people prefer to date (Berscheid & Walster, 1974b; Walster, Aronson, Abrahams, & Rottman, 1966). It appears, however, that in reality people partially choose others on the degree of match between their levels of physical attractiveness (Berscheid, Dion, Walster, & Walster, 1971; Huston, 1973), presumably because matching increases the likelihood of acceptance on the part of the other. Other desirable stimulus characteristics that would suggest potential future rewardingness of the partner may be inferred from the reputation, behavior, and appearance of the other during this initial stage. Again the degree of match in these stimulus characteristics is evaluated. A positive assessment of future rewardingness induces comparisons of values, broadly defined to include attitudes, beliefs, needs, etc., in the next stage.

At the *value* comparison stage, people begin the process of assessing the degree of congruence in value-related areas. This assessment is seen to come from increasing self-disclosure between the pair, although topics of self-disclosure may be at general levels, such as leisure interests, religious beliefs, and/or attitudes toward politics. Disclosure of more intimate topics is possible at this stage, but likely proceeds in slow increments in order to decrease the risk involved in revealing extremely intimate details of oneself. Although the role stage has not yet been reached, self-disclosure allows some comparison of role compatibility in the value stage. Those roles (friend, wage-earner, etc.) that must be assessed through extensive interaction and time together cannot be accurately determined at this value comparison stage, however. The impetus to move to the next stage comes from awareness by the partners that their value similarity is indicative of mutual goals for the relationship.

The *role* stage involves a determination by the partners as to the compatibility of the roles that each will play in the continuing relationship. Role is defined by Murstein (1976) in a broader sense than standard sociological conceptions. Essentially, *role* in this model refers to the expectations that individuals have for their partners as to how they may function in their potential marriage. This conception views role from a more individualistic perspective. This stage occurs last due to the more intimate nature of the behaviors indicative of role compatibility. Such behaviors cannot be observed at earlier, less intimate stages.

A more recent reformulation (Murstein, 1987) holds that stimulus, value, and role factors all operate throughout the course of courtship, although one factor predominates at a given time, mainly dependent on the extent of interaction between partners. In other words, discovery of partner attributes at the role stage requires more interaction between partners than at the stimulus stage.

According to the model, successful completion of these three stages supposedly prepares couples for marriage, although some couples will continually work on the factors that define each stage. On the other hand, Murstein (1976) acknowledged that some couples will marry without going through the complete sequence.

Lewis's Premarital Dyadic
Formation Framework (PDF)

In this framework Lewis (1972, 1973a) proposed a general model of heterosexual relationship development based on six sequential processes. These processes, and how they are connected, were determined through previous empirical work in courtship. After conceptualizing the model, Lewis (1973a) followed premarital couples over time to assess the validity of his model. This model does not necessarily posit that all relationships that proceed through the six processes will eventuate in marriage. Lewis proposed, however, that all processes will be completed prior to the selection of a mate, although the final decision to marry may be based largely on situational, idiosyncratic factors. Each process gives rise to the next one, and the outcome of the succeeding process is dependent on successful completion of the preceding process.

The initial process is posited to involve *perceiving similarities*. Specifically, perceived similarity in the areas of sociocultural background, value consensus, interests, and personality is particularly important. Some of these perceptions (e.g., approximate age, etc.) can come from mere observation, while others (e.g., interests, values, personality) are more accurately assessed through direct interaction with the other.

The second sequential process is *achieving pair rapport*. This process is facilitated by the prior perception of similarity, which, in turn, facilitates the expression of positive feelings. Thus rapport is induced through ease of communication, positive evaluation of the other, satisfaction with the pair relationship, and perceived validation of the self. It should be noted that these subprocesses indicative of rapport are a combination of perceptions, emotions, and behaviors.

The third sequential process is *inducing self-disclosure*, which again is thought to be facilitated by the previous process of rapport building. When partners feel rapport with each other, they should be more likely to reveal more intimate personal details. Self-disclosure eliminates or lessens the idealization characteristic of early relationships, thus allowing people to self-disclose even more.

The fourth sequential process is *role-taking*. The previous stage of self-disclosure allows the pair to be empathic with each other, thus facilitating the ability of each to place him or herself in the other's role. Lewis (1972) acknowledged that the possible efficacy of role-taking in facilitating premarital development may be contingent on other factors such as gender and differences in characteristics of the partners.

The fifth process in the sequential model is *achieving interpersonal role-fit*. No explanation is given by Lewis (1972) as to how the previous process of role-taking influences this process, although it would seem important for people to be able to put themselves in another's role before they could determine how well they might mesh with the other person. Role-fit is seen to be achieved through at least three subprocesses: observed personality similarity, role complementarity, and need complementarity. Lewis (1972), however, posited that the pattern of role-fit can differ between couples, with some preferring role complementarity and others preferring the other two types of fit.

The final process is *achieving dyadic crystallization*, which has ostensibly been facilitated by successful completion of the preceding processes. Dyadic crystallization is marked by progressive involvement, dyadic functioning, boundary establishment, pair commitment, and couple identity formation. The gist of these subprocesses is that the individuals in the relationship become increasingly interdependent as they develop an identity as a couple with a commitment toward more permanency. Such permanency may take the form of either a continuing premarital relationship or eventual marriage.

Critique of stage models. Although the stage models may have intuitive appeal, they suffer from several shortcomings. First, some of these models are based on questionable assumptions and a lack of conceptual clarity regarding the sequential processes. Implicit in the sequential models is the premise that premarital relationships are highly intimate, with extensive communication of feelings, attitudes, and values. Such communication would be essential for partners to ascertain such things as role-fit, value similarity, commitment, etc. Two well-known studies cast doubt on this assumption, at least for some segments of the population. Cuber and Harroff's (1966) study of marriage suggested that a substantial number of marital relationships lack intimacy, even from the beginning of the relationship. "Passive-congenial" couples in this study were very low in intimacy behaviors beginning in premarriage. A more recent study (Rubin, 1976) found that working-class couples' premarital relationships tended to move to marriage by rather nonintimate events such as a difficult home environment or unwanted pregnancy. These motivators do not suggest a close inspection of partners' attributes or communication between partners.

One major conceptual weakness of some sequential models is a lack of rationale for why particular stages or processes precede or follow other stages (Rubin & Levinger, 1974). For example, it is unclear why value comparison must precede role considerations in

Murstein's (1976) SVR model. In fact, Levinger and Snoek (1972) make a convincing theoretical case that couples use socially defined roles in the beginning stages of a relationship, rather than later. On balance, it should be noted that Murstein (1987) has done some theoretical reformulation of the SVR model by suggesting that stimulus, value, and role information are gathered throughout the relationship, but some factors will predominate and accelerate faster at particular stages due to more extensive interaction between partners. Murstein (1987) suggested, however, that the stimulus stage occurs in the first encounter, the value stage is from the second to seventh encounters, and the role stage begins at the eighth encounter and beyond. These boundaries seem quite arbitrary and have little theoretical justification (Leigh, Holman, & Burr, 1987).

Another criticism of sequential models addresses methodological and statistical aspects of the studies on which the models are based. Murstein's (1976) data were mainly cross-sectional and did not allow for analyses that would determine a temporal ordering of stages (cf. Rubin & Levinger, 1974). The test of Lewis' (1973a) PDF model did not use more advanced statistical techniques (path analyses, structural equation modeling, etc.) that could uncover causal pathways.

Additionally, a problem with the sequential stage models is that there are no studies that replicate the results used to develop these models. One attempt (Levinger, Senn, & Jorgensen, 1970) to replicate Kerckhoff and Davis' (1962) filter model found that courtship progress was not predicted by either similarity or need complementarity, and length of the relationship did not mediate the influence of these variables. Similarly, as discussed earlier, there is little empirical support for the theory of complementary needs, a theory that plays a central role in three of the sequential models. Recently one short longitudinal study (Leigh et al., 1987) failed to replicate Murstein's findings, although Murstein (1987) pointed out several deficiencies in this replication attempt.

Another criticism of these models is that they do not accurately portray the likely complexity of the mate-selection process. These models assume that compatibility between partners on individual characteristics is the primary moving force of movement to marriage. Such an assumption ignores other potential influences on courtship, such as the interaction between partners or external circumstances that propel people to marriage (Huston, Surra, Fitzgerald, & Cate, 1981).

A final criticism of these models relates to the constructs used to test compatibility and sequential processes. For example, it is not clear how such values concerning economic security, a place in the community, personality development, etc., as proposed by Farber (1957), would facilitate interpersonal interaction (Robins, 1985).

☙ The Interpersonal Process Model

Dissatisfaction with stage models that assumed the primacy of static variables (similarity, complementarity, rewards, etc.) in predicting mate-selection and the inability of such models to account adequately for movement to marriage led to the development of an *interpersonal process* model of premarital relationship development (Robins, 1983). This model assumes that social similarity, attitudinal similarity, and other static factors may play a role in the development of relationships, especially early in the relationship. The model posits, however, that the actual interaction within relationships is of primary importance in shaping the pattern of development to commitment or marriage (cf. Duck & Sants, 1983). On the other hand, the interactional aspects of relationships are also tied in a reciprocal fashion to individual characteristics of the partners, relationship attributes, and the social and physical environment (Kelley, Berscheid, Christensen, Harvey, Huston, Levinger, McClintock, Peplau, & Peterson, 1983).

The assumption of the interpersonal process model that relationships are shaped by different levels of causes (e.g., social environment) and to the unique interaction of the partners suggests that multiple pathways exist in the progression to commitment or marriage. Surra (1990) describes this model as one of *gradual differentiation*, where relationships have periods of stability, instability, growth, and decline. Change in relationships is continuous with no clearly demarcated stages of development. This view does allow for different pathways to marriage, although the assumption is that some common developmental patterns can be found. This view of relationship development contrasts with one of *early determinism* (Surra, 1990), which assumes that early relationship features work throughout the course of the relationship to determine stability or other relationship states. Supposedly such changes describe development for all couples. Research in support of this position (viz., Berg & McQuinn, 1986) will be presented in the next chapter.

At least one early study of courtship (Bolton, 1961) lends support to the idea of different pathways to marriage. Bolton (1961) identified, on the basis of extensive interviews with a small sample of newlyweds, five types of developmental processes that can characterize the movement to marriage. The *personality meshing type* is conceptually related to the sequential models. It focused on personality "fit" and couples who fit this type tended to be similar in background and values. The *expediency-centered* type is characterized by a strongly felt pressure to marry by one or both partners. The pressure to marry usually comes out of some personality problem or identity crisis. These couples usually moved to marriage fairly rapidly if pressure was felt early in the relationship, or through sharp turning points if pressure occurred later in the courtship. The *identity clarification* relationship is focused on clarifying the identities of the interactants. Issues related to identity emerged through interaction, with increasing convergence of partners' ideas about roles in the relationship. The *relation centered* type is characterized by initial superficial commitment. Over time, however, commitment builds through adjustments, shared understandings, etc. On the other hand, these courtships can be fragile, with ups and downs, misunderstandings, outside influences, etc. The *pressure and intrapersonal* relationship type is quite complex. Partners were rather similar in background, although partners' personalities did not complement each other. One partner was likely to push for commitments or marriage, while the other resisted such pressure, although the partners disliked open conflict. Much of the activity in the relationship is focused on mental activity to determine the suitability of the partner, fantasy, and maneuvering. Attraction in this type tended to be toward the relationship, rather than the partner.

More recently, other researchers (Cate, Huston, & Nesselroade, 1986; Femlee, Sprecher, & Bassin, 1990; Surra, 1985, 1987) have framed their examination of the path to marriage from an interpersonal process perspective.

Retrospective Studies With the Interpersonal Process Model

One study (Cate et al., 1986) examined the movement from first meeting to marriage using retrospective reports from a sample of 50 newlywed couples. The progression to marriage was graphed separately by the partners on a "chance of marriage" graph from the start of their relationship until they were married. Questionnaires were then completed by each partner that assessed conflict, relationship maintenance, love, and ambivalence at casual, serious, committed, and marital levels of involvement. In accord with the assumption of the interpersonal process model that relationship causes exist at several levels, other questions asked about external factors that might have influenced the course of development (e.g., whether they had been seriously involved with someone else when they met their partner, objections from parents, whether they perceived having potential alternative partners when they married, etc.).

The graphical data (0% to 100% chance of marriage at each month in the relationship) were analyzed using a modified principal components analysis (Tucker, 1966). This analytical technique is more fully discussed in Cate et. al. (1986). The analysis identified three reference curves that represented the variation in the paths to marriage. Partners each received a score (similar to a factor score) that was indicative of how similar their graphs were to one of the reference curves. To visually illustrate the developmental shape of these pathways, Figure 3.1 shows the average curve for each of the three representative pathways to marriage. Correlations were then performed between the scores for each pathway and conflict, maintenance behaviors, love, ambivalence, and indicators of the external factors.

The prolonged courtship. Scores on Path 1, which has a slow, up-and-down progression to marriage (the "prolonged" path), were positively correlated with conflict at all premarital stages and with

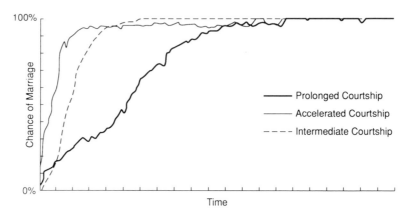

Figure 3.1. Pathways to Marriage

ambivalence during serious dating. Scores on this path also correlated negatively with age at time of meeting the spouse and with the
perception that parents were eager for the participant to marry. The
increased levels of conflict and ambivalence may contribute to the
turbulent movement of these courtships, while on the other hand,
the parental opposition noted in these types may increase conflict
and ambivalence.

The accelerated courtship. Path 2 moved rapidly to asymptote, then
dropped off somewhat (the "accelerated" path). Participant scores
on Path 2 correlated negatively with conflict and marginally negatively with maintenance at serious dating. Unlike on Path 1, higher
scores on Path 2 correlated positively with age at the time of meeting
the spouse and with eagerness of the parents for the participant to
marry. These findings paint a picture of the accelerated courtship as
one that had lower conflict and maintenance as partners become serious, thus enhancing the likelihood of compatible interaction between
partners. Such compatibility may have moved them to commitment.
On the other hand, events external to the relationship, such as being
relatively older at the time of meeting the spouse, and the perception
that parents approve of the partner, may set the stage for quick
movement to commitment.

The intermediate courtship. Path 3 was characterized by relatively slow movement to asymptote at the beginning of the relationship, followed by a moderate ascent to commitment that fell between the other two paths (the "intermediate" path). Scores on this path were negatively related to conflict throughout all courtship phases, such that the closer resemblance to Path 3, the lower the conflict. Similarly, there was a tendency for scores on this path to correlate negatively with ambivalence at serious dating. There was a positive association between Path 3 scores and age at the time of meeting the spouse and serious involvement with another person at the time participants met their marital partners. These findings characterized intermediate courtships as low in conflict, but with initial hesitancy and somewhat slow movement to commitment. This initial hesitancy may be due to people in such paths having a relatively greater number of prior relationships and having been more likely to be involved in a serious relationship at the time of meeting the present partner. Issues of disengaging from a prior relationship could result in a hesitancy to become involved in a new relationship.

This study (Cate et al., 1986) examined various levels of causality, but did not allow definitive identification of causal factors in the variation of movement to marriage because alternative explanations for the results were not systematically explored. Congruent with the interpersonal process model, however, the study did suggest that the interaction between partners (conflict, maintenance behaviors), individual attributes or processes (ambivalence), and factors external to the relationship (parental eagerness for participant to marry, age at meeting spouse, etc.) may act together to help shape the progression of mate selection.

The interpersonal process approach to examining variations in courtship patterns has been examined in two other studies (Surra, 1985, 1987) that used a retrospective methodology. These studies also used a graphing procedure and newlywed couples as in the Cate et al. (1986) study, except that data were also gathered on (a) affectional, instrumental, and leisure activities of the couple; and (b) reasons for changes in commitment over the course of the courtship. Results of the studies (Surra, 1985, 1987) uncovered four courtship pathways similar to those in the Cate et al. (1986) study; three of the paths replicated Cate et al.'s (1986) accelerated, intermediate, and prolonged courtships. The fourth path was similar to the accelerated courtship but had a downturn in commitment late in its progression (called an *accelerated-arrested* path). Differences in activities with the partner and social network members were found between the four paths (Surra, 1985). Partners (as a group) became more active with each other over time and less active with their social networks, although this withdrawal happened to a greater extent and more rapidly for the accelerated-arrested couples than for the accelerated ones. In addition, those in prolonged relationships became relatively less interdependent with their partners over time but maintained their level of activity with their network relative to those in other paths. Those in the intermediate type differed from those in the other paths by having more network activity and less companionship with the partner.

Differences in activities of courting couples are paralleled by differences in the reasons individuals in different paths give for why their relationships changed over time in level of commitment (Surra, 1987). Reasons for change in commitment were classified as intra-personal/normative, dyadic, social network, or circumstantial reasons. Intrapersonal/normative reasons are those that refer to either partner's normative beliefs about the timing or circumstances of marriage, the suitability of the partner as a potential mate, or the attractiveness of marriage. Dyadic reasons consist of those that refer to behavior between partners or to attributions about the nature of the partner or the relationship. Social network reasons are those that denote something about the actual interaction, projected interaction, or attributions concerning friends, kin, other partners, and significant others. Circumstantial reasons refer to predictable or random external happenings over which the individual has no or limited control. Those in prolonged paths reported more dyadic (e.g., self-disclosure, conflict, etc.) and circumstantial (e.g., luck, end of school year, etc.) reasons for changes in their courtships, probably due to their increased length. On the other hand, those in accelerated courtships mentioned proportionately more intrapersonal/normative (e.g., personal predispositions, normative standards about courtship, etc.)

and circumstantial reasons for changes in their commitment to marry than did the other types.

The interpersonal process studies discussed above looked retrospectively at courtships that ended in marriage. Despite the obvious problems with retrospective studies, the above studies did illuminate important processes in courtship. Studying only relationships that end in marriage, however, does not yield information on why some couples marry and others do not. The ideal study would examine couples from first meeting to either breakup or marriage and then determine the factors that predict stability. In practice, the usual procedure is to follow dating couples over a relatively short time period, usually a few months, and then look for factors that differentiate stable from unstable relationships. Again, this method is not ideal because some stable couples in such studies will likely break up before marriage occurs. This methodology seems to be the most practical alternative, however, given the large monetary costs and logistical difficulties encountered in following couples from the beginning of their relationships to the date of marriage. One recent study (Femlee et al., 1990) has used the interpersonal process framework to uncover some of the factors at multiple levels of analysis that may affect relationship stability.

A Prospective Study With the Interpersonal Process Model

For approximately 13 weeks Femlee et al. (1990) followed more than 400 students involved in a premarital relationship. The participants were initially assessed for their status on variables at the individual, dyadic, and social environment levels. These individuals then were asked at the follow-up whether they were still together, and, if not together, when they broke up. This study did not examine how relationships differ in their progression to marriage, one aspect of the interpersonal process model. These researchers wanted to examine how constructs at different levels of analysis might affect the development of relationships.

Some factors at all the levels of analysis predicted relationship breakup, for example, love, maintenance behaviors, ambivalence, sexual intimacy, comparison level for alternatives, time spent together, etc. (Femlee et al., 1990). Stability was positively related to time spent together (dyadic variable), comparison level for alternatives (dyadic variable), and partners' social support (social network variable), while being an interracial couple (dyadic variable) was related to less stability. Interestingly, no individual variables were related to stability of these relationships.

❧ Conclusions

Theoretical views of courtship have evolved over time with the development of models that reflect an increasing awareness that the process of mate choice is a complex process. The features of these models also have mirrored a change over time in mate selection that has moved from relatively familial and societal control to personal control of choice. Early theories (i.e., Freudian) focused on factors related to individuals' past history with their parents that might predict mate choice. These theories were inadequate in accounting for progress to marriage by individuals.

The subsequent models of courtship moved from examining unconscious motivational factors taken from Freudian theory to examining the compatibility of partners' personal needs and attitudes. These models assumed that people make conscious, rational decisions about whom they wish to marry. Models that postulated that similarity was a selection factor were questioned on conceptual grounds. The complementary needs model (Winch, 1955a) suffered from a lack of empirical support.

Stage models that postulated a sequence of factors (e.g., similarity in values, complementarity, role compatibility) to operate during the courtship period to propel people to marriage were developed next. These models were found inadequate on the basis of conceptual and methodological problems as well as a lack of replication.

Presently those adhering to an interpersonal process model of courtship are more likely to acknowledge that partners' behavioral interactions help shape the development of premarital relationships. At the same time the interpersonal process model acknowledges that causes of mate choice can exist at several levels, that is, individual, dyadic, social environment, and physical environment (Kelley et al., 1983). This perspective has shed some light on the multiple factors that may influence the various paths to marriage, as well as uncovering several factors at different levels of analysis that may promote stability in premarital relationships.

Despite these advances in our understanding of courtship, our knowledge of the mate-selection process is still quite rudimentary. Several findings show that people tend to marry those who are similar to themselves (cf., Burgess & Wallin, 1953; Hendrick, 1981), probably because societal structure limits our opportunity to associate with people significantly different from ourselves (Kerckhoff, 1974). So this narrowing of the field of eligibles is not likely due to conscious decision processes. We know little about the processes that follow this initial matching. Given that Robins (1985) found that people may seriously date only a few partners, it would not appear that people make extensive searches for compatible partners. So if partners do not engage in active selection processes, the question becomes, "What are the factors that facilitate partners' adaptation to each other over time?" Although studying the entire courtship experience from first meeting to marriage is ideal, this has not been done. We have discussed in this chapter some proposed models that try to account for the entire course to commitment. We now turn to research that examines the individual, dyadic, social network, and circumstantial factors that have been identified by various studies to promote stability in premarital relationships over relatively short periods of time.

4

Factors Predicting Premarital Relationship Stability

Scholars have long been fascinated by the study of courtship and all its attendant features. Although the development of theory concerning "who will marry whom" has been hampered at times by conceptual and theoretical challenges, researchers have nevertheless pursued the study of courtship with a vengeance! Literally hundreds of studies have been conducted on love, commitment, social exchange characteristics, conflict, and communication in premarital relationships. Most of these studies do not examine courtship per se, yet they are highly informative concerning the factors that influence the development, happiness, and stability of premarital pairings. In this chapter we examine only the recent studies that have followed individuals or couples over time.

We feel that the work done on the interpersonal process model of courtship is useful in identifying factors at various levels of analysis that may influence the course of developing courtships or predict the stability of premarital relationships. Surra (1987) has identified four primary levels of analysis that are applicable to the study of interpersonal relationships: individual, dyadic, social network, and circumstantial. In the current chapter we utilize Surra's framework as an organizing tool. We have expanded this framework slightly by including three areas in our definition of dyadic factors. These include: (a) relationship states that can be assessed to a large extent only by the partners themselves (commitment, love, etc.); (b) aspects of actual interaction that can be reported by the partners and/or by outside observers (conflict, self-disclosure, etc.); and (c) psychological or social attributes between partners (dyadic pattern) that can only be assessed objectively by outside observers (e.g., attitude similarity, similarity in attractiveness, etc.). We use this framework as our guide in reviewing those factors that predict premarital relationship stability.

To minimize the likelihood of imputing importance to chance findings, in general, only predictors that have been examined in two or more studies are reviewed. These studies are listed in Table 4.1. It should be noted that because this chapter is organized by type of predictor, the findings of most studies will be discussed under several headings.

It should be noted that although most of the literature conceptualizes the causes of stability from a unidirectional perspective, causality from the interpersonal process view is likely reciprocal in many cases. In addition, in many instances the factors may not be independent of each other. In very few studies has such overlap been statistically controlled; nor has the literature emphasized the study of multiple factors simultaneously. When applicable, we will point out when variables were compared within a study as to their unique ability to predict breakup.

❧ Individual Factors

Individual factors, as we define them, are those factors that denote something that is characteristic or dispositional about either

Table 4.1 Major Longitudinal Studies of Premarital Stability: Variables Reviewed in Chapter 4

Studies	Close[a]	Comt[b]	Comn[c]	CL-Alt[d]	Con[e]	Eq[f]	Int[g]	Inv[h]	Lv[i]	Rew[j]	Sat[k]	Sex[l]	SE[m]	Sim[n]	SN[o]
							Variables								
Berg & McQuinn (1986)			X	X	X	X			X	X	X				
Berscheid et al. (1989)	X				X	X	X		X	X	X				
Cate et al. (1985)						X				X					
Femlee et al. (1990)		X		X	X	X	X	X	X			X	X	X	X
Hendrick et al. (1988)		X	X			X		X	X		X		X		
Hill et al. (1976)	X	X					X		X			X		X	
Lloyd (1990)					X										
Lewis (1973)															X
Lloyd et al. (1984)	X	X		X						X	X				
Lujansky & Mikula (1983)						X					X				
Lund (1985)		X						X	X	X					
Parks & Adelman (1983)							X		X					X	X
Rusbult (1983)		X		X				X		X	X				
Simpson (1987)	X			X							X				
Sprecher (1987)			X									X			
Sprecher & Femlee (1991)															X
Stephen (1984b)		X									X				
Surra & Longstreth (1990)			X		X		X							X	

NOTE: Only variables used in two or more studies are included.
[a] closeness; [b] commitment; [c] communication; [d] comparison level for alternatives; [e] conflict; [f] equity; [g] interaction frequency; [h] investments; [i] love; [j] rewards; [k] satisfaction; [l] sexual involvement; [m] self-esteem; [n] similarity; [o] social network

partner in a relationship. These factors include personality characteristics, preferences for activities, attitudes, emotional reactions,
needs, and many others. Although classic personality characteristics have not fared well as predictors of relationship phenomena in
most studies (Huston & Levinger, 1978), some studies have begun
to examine those individual factors that might be more pertinent to
interpersonal relations. In general, however, these too have not been
particularly potent in predicting stability in relationships. Isolated
findings suggest that stability is predicted by: (a) being low in self-
monitoring, (b) ease of being oneself in a relationship (Femlee et al.,
1990), (c) a female partner who has a preference for relationship
maintenance activities (Surra & Longstreth, 1990), and (d) a male
partner who has a low Hope for Power (Stewart & Rubin, 1974).
Adopting a conservative orientation toward sexual involvement is
predictive of instability (Simpson, 1987).

Self-esteem is the only individual variable that has been used in
more than one study to predict relationship stability. Hendrick,
Hendrick, and Adler (1988) followed 30 couples over a 2-month period.
Self-esteem (assessed by asking participants about self-feelings and
present happiness) discriminated stable from unstable couples. On
the other hand, Femlee et al. (1990) did not find that self-esteem
predicted the stability of the relationships of 447 individuals followed over a 12-week to 13-week period. In summary, there is some
growing evidence that individual variables may play a role in relationship stability. Replication of past studies and identification of potentially salient individual variables, however, need to be undertaken.

⭐ Dyadic States, Interaction, and Patterns

The term "dyadic" is used here to emphasize the fact that these
factors exist only if there is a relationship between two people. *Dyadic
states* are those that refer to social psychological phenomena that
arise out of a relationship between people but may be held by only
one member of a couple. For example, due to their history together,
John may love Mary, although Mary may not love John. Other exam-
ples of dyadic states are such phenomena as commitment and satis-

faction. *Dyadic interactions* are those behaviors that occur between individuals in a relationship, for example, conflict, self-disclosure. *Dyadic patterns* are factors that are derived from the degree of match between individual attributes of each partner in a relationship. For example, attitude similarity is derived from the degree to which each partner's attitudes mirror those of the other partner.

Dyadic States

Love. In everyday life love is seen as the characteristic that defines functional close relationships. It is not surprising that love has been examined relatively extensively as a predictor of stability in premarital relations. Although love is recognized as an important aspect of close relationships, there is much discussion as to what constitutes the phenomenon of love. Love has been viewed as an attitude (Rubin 1970, 1973), an emotion (Berscheid & Walster, 1974a), attachment (Hazan & Shaver, 1987), and as a combination of some of these (Hatfield & Sprecher, 1986; Sternberg, 1986). Others conceptualize the phenomenon as "styles of loving" (Hendrick & Hendrick, 1986; Lee, 1973). (See Hendrick and Hendrick, 1992, for a complete treatment of love in relationships.)

Love has been found in several studies to predict the stability of premarital relationships. One commonly used measure is the well-known, psychometrically sound measure by Rubin (1970, 1973). This nine-item instrument is made up of three components: attachment (e.g., "If I were lonely, my first thought would be to seek (partner) out"), caring (e.g., "If (partner) were feeling badly, my first duty would be to cheer him (or her) up"), and intimacy (e.g., "I feel that I can confide in (partner) about virtually everything").

Hill, Rubin, and Peplau (1976) were the first to show that Rubin's measure of love predicted the stability of premarital couples in their classic longitudinal Boston Couples Study of 231 couples who were followed over a 2- year period. Not surprisingly, those individuals who reported the highest levels of love initially were more likely to be together 2 years later. This finding held for both men and women.

Lund (1985) used the Rubin (1970, 1973) love measure, along with other variables (commitment, investments, rewards), to predict premarital relationship continuance over a 4-month period in a sample of 129 university students. Results showed again that love discriminated between stable and unstable couples. The results, however, showed that love did not significantly predict breakup after investment and commitment were controlled. This finding may be due to the fact that both love and commitment are measuring some similar relationship qualities in this sample, such that love was not a unique predictor when compared with commitment. The relationship between love and commitment will be discussed later in this chapter.

Two other longitudinal studies (Berg & McQuinn, 1986; Femlee et al., 1990) used a measure of love devised by Braiker and Kelley (1979) to predict premarital stability. This 10-item measure was developed from an analysis of items gleaned from married couples' retrospective reports of the nature of their relationships during dating. The scale taps multiple aspects of love, some of which parallel those in the Rubin scale. The scale taps feelings of attachment, belonging, closeness, sexual involvement, commitment, and uniqueness of the relationship, but does not include items related to self-disclosure and caring, as does the Rubin scale. The Braiker and Kelley (1979) love scale also has the ability to predict premarital breakup.

Berg and McQuinn (1986) followed 38 couples from quite early in their relationships until approximately 4 months later. Their study looked at general measures of relationship qualities and specific social exchange variables as predictors of stability. Initial levels of love did discriminate between stable and unstable relationships. In addition, love increased significantly over time for intact couples but not for those who had broken up.

Femlee et al. (1990) also used the Braiker and Kelley (1979) love measure, along with other Braiker and Kelley measures, to examine the stability of the relationships. The Braiker and Kelley scale of love was modified slightly due to a factor analysis of this scale. The revised scale eliminated a sexuality item in the original scale but added an item on self-disclosure by the participant to the partner. As with previous studies, love was a significant predictor of breakup.

Only one study (Hendrick et al., 1988) has examined the ability of different types of love, or styles of loving, to predict relationship stability. The styles of loving were first identified by Lee (1973), and

Hendrick and Hendrick (1986) have developed the Love Attitudes Scale to assess individuals' scores on the different styles. These styles are: (a) Erotic love (romantic, passionate, disclosing verbally and physically); (b) Ludic love (playful, lack of commitment to partner, avoidance of involvement); (c) Storgic love (muted emotional disclosure, love slow in developing, physical intimacy not essential to relationship stability); (d) Manic love (ambivalent, possessive and dependent); (e) Pragmatic love (sensible, practical, low emotionality); and (f) Agapic love (giving, other-centered, caring). Again love was predictive of relationship stability. Individuals in intact couples reported higher levels of erotic love and lower levels of ludic love than those who had broken up. So it appears that relationship stability may be positively affected by love styles that are romantic, passionate, disclosing, involved, and committed.

Based on these studies, courtship development is enhanced through love that is characterized by a: (a) need to care for the partner; (b) feeling of attachment to the partner; (c) feeling of commitment; (d) feeling that the partner can be disclosed to and, in fact, is disclosed to; (e) feeling of uniqueness about the relationship; (f) feeling of belonging, closeness, and involvement; and (g) feeling of being sexually involved. As will be shown in the remainder of this chapter, however, some of these characteristics have been studied as separate dimensions of relationships.

Commitment. The above discussion indicated that conceptions of love frequently view commitment as a part of love. This question has been addressed from both theoretical and empirical perspectives. Kelley (1983) argued from a theoretical perspective that love and commitment overlap considerably but that each factor has some unique features. Fehr (1988) presented empirical data in support of Kelley's stance. On the other hand, Sternberg (1986) posited that commitment is one of three components of love. Despite the conceptual ambiguities concerning commitment, several studies address how various measures of commitment are related to the stability of premarital relationships.

From a theoretical perspective, Johnson (1985) provided one of the most comprehensive conceptualizations of commitment. Johnson

(1985) pointed out that commitment can be broken down into two types: personal commitment to the partner and the relationship (personal dedication to remain) and structural commitment (commitment induced by constraints external to the relationship). Personal commitment involves attraction to the partner, attraction to the relationship, definition of self in terms of the relationship, and a moral obligation to continue the relationship. Structural commitment consists of irretrievable investment, social pressure to remain in the relationship, difficulty in ending the relationship, and dissatisfaction with available alternatives. No longitudinal study has included all of these elements of commitment.

Rusbult (1983) examined commitment in an investment model of relationships based on social exchange theory (Thibaut & Kelley, 1959). This model takes into account relationship rewards and costs, one's comparison level (i.e., the level of rewards a person is accustomed to receiving), one's comparison level for alternatives (i.e., the highest level of rewards a person could get in another relationship), investment in the relationship, satisfaction and commitment. Commitment is viewed as being predicted by high levels of satisfaction (rewards minus costs), high investment in the relationship, and a perception of relatively few alternative partners. Rusbult (1983) reported that high rewards, high investment, and low alternatives predicted commitment, although costs did not. Rusbult (1983) also examined the ability of commitment to differentiate those who stayed in relationships from those who broke up over a 7-month period. The concept of commitment was measured by calculating the mean of five questions concerning the length of time participants wanted the relationship to last, how attached they were to the partner, generally how committed they were to the partner, how likely it was that they would end the relationship, and how attractive an alternative partner would have to be for them to leave the present relationship. It should be noted that this assessment did not differentiate between personal and structural commitment. In addition, it included aspects of attachment, a concept that was included in some measurements of love. Nevertheless, commitment increased significantly over the 7 months for those in intact relationships, whereas commitment decreased for those who ended their relationships.

When commitment was compared with rewards, costs, alternatives, and investment as a unique predictor, it was the best predictor among that set of variables. A series of follow-up studies (Johnson & Rusbult, 1989) suggested that commitment is an important predictor of stability because highly committed people tend to devalue their alternatives over time, especially when the alternatives are highly attractive.

Lund (1985) developed a scale to measure commitment and compared its ability, in conjunction with relationship investments, to predict stability in relationships. Lund (1985) attempted to eliminate as much overlap as possible between her measure of commitment and Rubin's (1973) Love Scale by eliminating highly correlated items. The resulting instrument still correlated highly with love, congruent with Kelley's (1983) theoretical argument that the two concepts should overlap substantially. The Lund measure mixes personal commitment items (e.g., "How likely is it that your relationship will be permanent?") with structural commitment items (e.g., "How much trouble would ending your relationship be to you personally?"). Additionally, the scale directly asks how committed the person and the partner are to the relationship, as well as the availability of alternative partners. This longitudinal study found that commitment and investments significantly discriminated between stable and unstable relationships. Stable couples had higher commitment scores.

Hendrick et al. (1988) examined commitment as a predictor of stability using a modified version of the Lund (1985) instrument. This version assessed the participants' estimates of the relationship continuing and their own and their partner's commitment to the relationship. Thus this conception mainly taps *personal commitment*. Results of this longitudinal study found that personal commitment did discriminate between stable and unstable relationships. The higher the commitment, the higher the stability.

Three other studies (Hill et al., 1976; Lloyd, Cate, & Henton, 1984; Stephen, 1984b) measured commitment by asking study participants to report the "probability of marriage," the "probability that the current relationship will last for the next 10 years," or the "chance of marriage" in their relationships. It is unclear whether this measure taps personal or structural commitment or both. Findings of these studies are congruent with those already reviewed.

Hill et al. (1976) found that participants' perceptions of the probability of marriage (expressed as a percentage) when they were first contacted differentiated between intact and dissolved relationship. Couples who were still together at the follow-up reported higher probability of marriage than those in relationships that dissolved.

The measure of "chance of marriage" (0% to 100%) that taps commitment has been used in one study (Lloyd et al., 1984). In this study 131 individuals were initially surveyed, with 111 of those recontacted at 3 months, and 48 individuals contacted 7 months later. Chance of marriage was found to discriminate significantly between stable and unstable relationships after controlling for prior length of relationship, with those in stable relationships reporting higher initial chance of marriage.

To predict relationship continuity, Stephen (1984b) examined the utility of a commitment measure that asked respondents to estimate the probability that they would be with their partners in 10 years. He followed 130 couples at 6-week intervals for a 6-month period. At final follow-up 30 couples had ended their relationship. This probability measure of commitment predicted stability, with those in stable relationships reporting higher initial levels of commitment.

These studies suggest that commitment is an important element in the stability of premarital relationships. Generally personal commitment successfully predicted relationship stability. One study (Lund, 1985) that used a combined measure of personal and structural commitment also discriminated between stable and unstable relationships. No studies, however, examined only structural commitment. Several studies illustrated the ability of "probability of marriage" or "chance of marriage" measures of commitment to predict premarital stability.

Some of these studies do illuminate the unique role of commitment vis-à-vis other potentially overlapping constructs (e.g., length of relationship, rewards, costs, alternatives, and investments). These studies, however, do not examine those factors that may be determinants of both commitment and its related constructs. This omission is particularly troublesome given the demonstrated overlap of commitment with love. Logically it could be expected that commitment induced by structural constraints would have more negative consequences for the individual and the relationship than would personal commitment. In the following discussions some light may be shed on these questions through findings concerning the concepts of comparison level for alternatives and relationship satisfaction.

Comparison level for alternatives. The concept of comparison level for alternatives comes from social exchange theory (Thibaut & Kelley, 1959). It is defined as the level of outcomes or rewards that a person could receive from his or her best alternative to the present relationship. These potential alternatives can be other partners or alternative situations that do not include another partner. According to social exchange theory, the comparison level for alternatives partially determines the stability of a relationship. If one has a high comparison level for alternatives (both relationship and nonrelationship alternatives), the relationship should be less stable. Conversely, a low comparison level for alternatives should lead to stability. It should be clear from the previous discussion of commitment that comparison level for alternatives can be viewed as one component of structural commitment.

Rusbult (1983) was the first to examine comparison level for alternatives as a factor in premarital relationship stability (see earlier discussion of this study). Comparison level for alternatives was measured using two items that asked participants how appealing other potential dating partners were and how potential alternatives compared to their present partner. The findings showed that those who broke off their premarital relationships reported higher increases in their comparison level for alternatives over time than those who remained together. When comparison level for alternatives was compared with commitment, rewards, costs, and investments, however, it was reduced in its ability to predict break up. This diminution in the predictive power of alternatives should be interpreted cautiously, given that this alternative measure is likely confounded with satisfaction (rewards minus costs in this study). Johnson (1985) pointed out that this particular measure of comparison level for alternatives (along with some others) was not totally independent of relationship satisfaction because it asks participants to estimate their alternatives relative to their present partners.

The Lloyd et al. (1984) study examined comparison level for alternatives as it differentiated intact and dissolved couples over time. The two-item measure of alternatives asked how easy or hard it would be for the participant to find another partner and how that new partner would compare with the present partner. In this study comparison level for alternatives did not significantly predict premarital dissolution after controlling for length of the relationship. The measurement of comparison level for alternatives in this study is also likely not independent of satisfaction because participants were asked about alternatives relative to the present partner. The lack of significance in this study, as compared with Rusbult (1983), may be due to the fact that it examined initial alternatives, whereas the Rusbult (1983) study examined change in alternatives over time. On the other hand, the fact that controlling for prior length of relationship eliminated the relation between alternatives and stability indicates a need to control for possible intervening or confounding variables (e.g., relationship length).

Berg and McQuinn (1986) also assessed the ability of alternative level to predict dissolution (see previous discussion of this study). Their measure asked participants to indicate how their present relationship compared with others they could have. Those who broke up during the study had higher comparison levels for alternatives at the beginning of the study than those who stayed together. Also, those in dissolved relationships reported a greater increase in alternatives over time than those who stayed together. This result meshes with the finding reported by Rusbult (1983), although similar methodological problems existed in this study.

A study by Simpson (1987) was the first to examine comparison level for alternatives in relation to salient variables other than length of relationship as predictors of relationship stability. In this study 222 individuals were followed over a 3-month period. Three separate measures were used to tap comparison level for alternatives: best alternative partner index, best imagined alternative partner index, and ease of finding an alternative partner index. Again these three measures are answered relative to the present partner, thus all included to some extent the degree of satisfaction with their partners. Consequently, the measures may not be "pure" assessments of alternatives. Analyses showed all three indices discriminated between stable and unstable relationships, with increases in each being associated with breaking up. When these indices were directly compared with other salient variables (e.g., satisfaction) in their ability to predict stability, however, additional unique variance was not accounted for. This outcome lends some support to suggestions that these alternative measures also tap satisfaction with the relationship.

One recent study (Femlee et al., 1990) examined comparison level for alternatives, along with other variables, as a predictor of premarital breakup. Again this measure also implicitly assessed satisfaction by asking participants to compare their present relationship with other relationship and nonrelationship alternatives. The alternatives measure, however, was directly compared with other predictors. Comparison level for alternatives did predict stability in the expected direction, even when other variables were taken into account. Satisfaction was not assessed in this study, thus the problem with the alternatives measure also measuring satisfaction was not addressed.

In summary, comparison level for alternatives predicted relationship stability in four of the five studies reviewed; however, when other important variables (e.g., rewards, length of relationship, satisfaction, etc.) were taken into account, alternatives tended to not predict relationship longevity. Consequently, the role of comparison level for alternatives is usually obscured because its measurement includes elements of satisfaction, which renders it an "impure" measure.

Relationship satisfaction. Satisfaction with relationships is one of the most commonly examined variables in the study of close relationships. Consequently, this variable has been used to predict stability in premarital relationships in several studies. The wide use of this variable, however, should *not* imply that there is general agreement as to how it should be measured. It has been noted that some standard measures of satisfaction (e.g., the Dyadic Adjustment Scale; Spanier, 1976) mix together items referring to both behaviors and evaluations of a partner (see Huston & Robins, 1982). Huston and Robins (1982) suggested that this is a questionable practice because most often one wants to see how behaviors relate to evaluations of the relationship; however, this criticism does not present much of a problem in the studies reviewed here. Only one study uses the Dyadic Adjustment Scale (Hendrick et al., 1988). It also should be noted that satisfaction can be viewed as one indicator of personal commitment (see Johnson, 1973), thus complicating studies that compare satisfaction with commitment measures, which many times include both personal and structural components as a predictors of breakup.

In the Rusbult (1983) study satisfaction was used to predict dissolution of relationships. Satisfaction was assessed using two questions that asked about the participants' attraction to and satisfaction with that relationship. Results showed that satisfaction increased more over time for those in intact relationships versus those that had dissolved. A comparison of relationship satisfaction with alternatives, investments, and commitment showed satisfaction to have unique power in predicting stability, although the report did not indicate if the unique contribution was statistically significant.

Lujansky and Mikula (1983) followed 92 males over a 5-month period to assess the ability of social exchange variables, plus others such as satisfaction, to differentiate stable from unstable relationships. Satisfaction with the relationship was assessed by asking participants to indicate how favorably they rated their partners on 28 attributes potentially important for steady dating relationships (honesty, faithfulness, warmth, ambition, etc.). Initial satisfaction with the relationship was significantly higher for stable relationships than for unstable ones.

Satisfaction did predict relationship stability in the study by Stephen (1984b), even after measures of commitment and geographical distance between partners were controlled. Satisfaction was measured with the Locke-Wallace Short Marital Adjustment Test (Locke & Wallace, 1959) that had been adapted for premarital relationships.

Hendrick et al. (1988) used the Dyadic Adjustment Scale (Spanier, 1976), a 32-item scale that assesses both general evaluations of the relationship and the incidence of various behaviors thought to covary with satisfaction (e.g., communication, conflict, etc.), to predict relationship stability. Participants in ongoing relationships had higher satisfaction than did those in relationships that ended.

In contrast to the other studies, satisfaction has been found less promising as a predictor of stability in three other studies. Lloyd et al. (1984) used a four-item measure of satisfaction developed by Austin (1974), which asked participants to indicate how happy, content, angry, and guilty they felt about their present relationship. After controlling for the length of time people had been dating before the initial assessment, satisfaction did not differentiate those who had ended their relationships from those who had not.

A single item asking directly about participants' satisfaction with the relationship also did not predict stability in the previously discussed study by Berg and McQuinn (1986). This finding may be accounted for due to the relatively short time that these couples had been dating. The modal number of dates was only five. At this early stage of the relationship, satisfaction would be based on a fairly small number of observations of the partner, thus yielding possibly unreliable estimates of satisfaction.

Another failure of relationship satisfaction to predict relationship continuance is reported by Simpson (1987). The assessment of satisfaction was done by asking participants to rate how satisfied they were with all attributes of their partners (physical attractiveness, trustworthiness, social status, etc.). Participants in intact relationships had higher levels of satisfaction than did those in dissolved ones; however, when other variables were included, such as length of relationship, exclusivity of the relationship, sexual nature of the relationship, etc., satisfaction did not predict stability. Again these findings suggest that the measurement of satisfaction may not be independent of other relationship variables, or that satisfaction is caused by some of these other constructs.

The results of studies on satisfaction are not greatly informative in our understanding of premarital relationship stability. There is considerable controversy over the utility of using satisfaction indices in the study of marriage. This controversy is multifaceted and cannot be adequately discussed here. The reader can consult Glenn (1990) for a review that addresses this issue. Nevertheless, there are several reasons why satisfaction may not be a good predictor of relationship stability. For example, satisfaction is normally measured by reports from individuals rather than at the dyadic level. Thus satisfaction may not be informative concerning the nature of the relationship between two individuals, but only the feelings of one partner in the relationship. Also satisfaction may tap rather momentary evaluations that are not useful in examining issues of longevity in relationships. Satisfaction may also be a component of or related to other concepts (e.g., length of relationship, commitment) such that it does not predict unique variance when directly compared with these other variables. The studies reviewed above would lend some credence to that explanation; however, when satisfaction was measured at multiple points in the relationship (e.g., Rusbult, 1983), it seemed to have unique predictive ability. It may be that if satisfaction is measured over time, it is better able to predict relationship continuance.

Investment. One additional concept used to predict relationship continuity is that of investment in the relationship. As with comparison level for alternatives and satisfaction, investments in relationships are seen by some writers as indicative of commitment to a relationship (Johnson, 1973; Rusbult, 1983). Rusbult's (1983) investment model posits that commitment is a function of high satisfaction, low level of alternatives, and high *investment* in the relationship. Investments are broken down into extrinsic investments (mutual friends, shared experiences, shared possessions, etc.) and intrinsic investments (time, effort, communication with partner, etc.) that will be lost if one finds another partner (Rusbult, 1983). The reader is referred to Johnson (1985) for a discussion of possible conceptual problems with this approach to investments.

Rusbult's (1983) study empirically examined the ability of investments to predict relationship stability. Investments were operationalized using the mean of two summed questions asking: (a) how much they had invested in the relationship, and (b) what they would have lost by ending the relationship. Those in stable relationships reported greater increases in investments over time than those who had split up. When investments were compared with commitment, alternatives, costs, and rewards, however, investments no longer were a unique predictor of breakup.

The study by Lund (1985) also examined how well investments predict relationship stability. Investments were measured by asking participants to indicate how much they had invested in their relationships in 26 different areas (e.g., buying gifts, sharing feelings, doing favors, changing career plans for partner's sake, etc.), thus providing a more specific assessment than in the Rusbult (1983) study. Investments did differentiate stable from unstable relationships over time; however, the uniqueness of investments was unclear in relation to love, rewards received, and commitment, given the type of statistical analysis used.

Unlike the previous studies, Hendrick et al. (1988) used a two-item measure of investment to discriminate stable from unstable relationships. These items asked for estimates of both the participants' investments and their partners' investments. Partners in continuing relationships reported higher total relationship investments than those whose relationships had ended.

The ability of investment to differentiate stable from unstable relationships was also examined in the Femlee et al. (1990) study. Those in stable relationships reported higher investments than those who had ended their relationships. Investment size was not a unique predictor of breakup, however, when it was compared with variables such as length of relationship, comparison level for alternatives, social support from partner, racial differences, and other variables. It seems logical that the longer relationships continue, the greater the number of investments partners make. Thus it is unclear whether it is the length of relationship or the investments in the relationship that induce stability. Future studies will want to include simultaneous analysis of investment with related concepts.

These studies showed that investments in a relationship do predict the stability of premarital pairings. Investments were a significant predictor of stability in every study reviewed; however, in those studies where variables were compared as unique predictors, investments lost their power to predict stability. One possible explanation for these findings is that investments may be a component of other dyadic variables, especially commitment.

Rewards. According to Rusbult's (1983) investment model, relationship rewards are predictive of relationship stability through their effect on relationship satisfaction. Reward level has been examined in several studies.

Rusbult (1983) assessed rewards using the mean of two summed items that asked how rewarding the participant's relationship was and how their present relationship compared to their ideal. This measure discriminated ongoing from dissolved relationships. Participants in stable relationships reported more growth in rewards over time than did those in unstable pairings. This finding was supported by the Lloyd et al. (1984) study in which individuals estimated rewards they received in the areas of love, money, goods, services, information, status (Foa & Foa, 1974), and sex. Higher initial rewards predicted relationship continuance, even after controlling for relationship length. In the Rusbult (1983) study, however, rewards were relatively weak in predicting stability when commitment, investments, alternatives, and costs were controlled.

Two studies have suggested that rewards may not effectively predict relationship continuance. Berg and McQuinn (1986) found that rewards (measured by two items asking about how much the partner (a) did favors and (b) helped them with problems) did not predict relationship stability. In addition, Lund (1985) found that rewards (measured with a 20-item scale of individual rewards) did not significantly predict breakup after controlling for commitment, love, and investments.

The bulk of evidence from these studies suggests that rewards do not uniquely predict relationship continuity. Rewards may not be independent of other concepts that are typically measured in these type of studies. Or it is certainly possible that rewards may precede the development of commitment and love, thus being a highly related, but separate construct.

Equity. Equity theory (Walster, Walster, & Berscheid, 1978), another elaboration of social exchange theory, has been touted as a general theory to explain interpersonal relationships and has been used to examine relationship stability. Relationships are said to be equitable when partners receive outcomes proportionate to their inputs. People are overbenefited when they receive more than they deserve and underbenefited when they receive less than they deserve. Although equity consistently predicts satisfaction in relationships (Cate, Lloyd, Henton, & Larson, 1982; Walster, Walster, & Traupmann, 1978), no studies have found equity to predict stability in relationships (e.g., Berg & McQuinn, 1986; Cate, Lloyd, & Henton, 1986; Femlee et al., 1990; Lujansky & Mikula, 1983) when other relationship variables are controlled.

Dyadic Interactions

Closeness or interdependence. Although many of the concepts discussed above might be viewed as indicative of "closeness" or "interdependence," this concept has been conceptualized and assessed in several ways. Closeness or interdependence has been equated with "involvement" in one study. Lloyd et al. (1984) conceptualized involvement or closeness using a scale developed by Levinger, Rands, and Talaber (1977). This scale taps the dimensions of the uniqueness of the relationship, disclosure, outcome correspondence, and emotional caring. So this conceptualization includes aspects of love (caring) and dyadic interaction (disclosure). Participants who were in intact versus dissolved relationships at both a 3-month and 7-month follow-up reported initially higher involvement, after controlling for length of prior acquaintance.

Hill et al. (1976) had their participants simply estimate on a Likert scale their perceived degree of closeness, thus allowing individuals to define closeness in their own manner. This conceptualization of closeness discriminated between those who broke up versus those who stayed together, with people in stable relationships reporting greater closeness. The obvious problem in allowing participants to define concepts for themselves is that it probably increases the likelihood that the conceptualizations will include considerable variation in what constitutes closeness.

The most extensive conceptualization of interdependence or closeness comes from the work of Berscheid, Snyder, and Omoto (1989). Their closeness measure is based on the "close relationships" framework developed by Kelley et al. (1983). Within this framework closeness consists of high frequency of interaction, high diversity of activities in which the couple engage, and strong impact of the partners on each other. A 27-item closeness measure has participants indicate the total number of minutes usually spent with the partner on a daily basis (frequency of interaction), the number of different activities done alone with the partner during the past week (diversity of interaction), and the extent to which the partners are affected or influenced by each other (strength of impact). Simpson (1987) used this measure in his longitudinal study; closeness did predict stability; however, when compared with other variables such as satisfaction, length of relationship, comparison level for alternatives, etc., closeness no longer was a unique predictor.

Using this measure, Berscheid et al. (1989) followed 74 individuals over a 9-month period. Their results showed that closeness was a significant predictor, when controlling length of relationship, subjective closeness, and hedonic emotional tone of the relationship. The question remains as to whether this measure would have been predictive of stability had other more salient variables (e.g., comparison level for alternatives, satisfaction, commitment) been included in the analysis.

It is unclear at this time how well closeness predicts relationship stability. The work by Berscheid et al. (1989) in conceptualizing and measuring closeness is a positive movement in identifying the salient features of relationship closeness; however, the empirical utility of the concept has yet to be demonstrated. A more fruitful approach may be to examine dyadic interactional concepts related to the various components of closeness identified by Berscheid et al. (1989) as they differentiate stable from unstable pairings. These concepts are discussed below.

Interaction frequency. Frequency of interaction has been examined in several studies. Hill et al. (1976) found that seeing the partner daily did not predict stability of relationships; however, three other studies have found support for higher frequency of interaction being related to relationship continuance. Two of these studies used more refined measures of frequency.

Parks and Adelman (1983) followed 172 people over a 3-month period. Measures of the amount of time spent talking face-to-face with the partner and the amount of leisure time spent together during the previous two weeks were gathered, along with social network and similarity variables. The amount of time spent with the partner was predictive of stability, even after controlling for uncertainty concerning the partner. The more time spent together, the more stable the relationships.

Surra and Longstreth (1990) examined whether frequency of activities engaged in by couples predicted stability over time. In this study 59 couples were followed over a one-year period. Data were collected in an initial interview and questionnaire session and by telephone at one-month intervals to assess the number of activities engaged in, conflict over those activities, and satisfaction with those activities during the preceding 2 weeks. The number of activities engaged in together discriminated stable from unstable couples, although prediction was better for women. The number of activities related to relationship maintenance (men only), food and errands, secure stimulation (e.g., reading), entertainment and cultural events, sports and games, and sexual interaction (for women only) was higher for stable couples compared to the unstable ones. The fact that several activity areas were predictive of stability also suggests that diversity of activities is important. No direct comparisons were made with other relevant relationship variables; however, a recent study has examined frequency of interaction as a unique predictor of relationship stability. Femlee et al. (1990) found that fewer hours spent together per week with the partner was predictive of breakup, after controlling for length of relationship, investments, comparison level for alternatives, and other variables. The more hours spent together, the more likely the relationship was to remain intact. The question concerning this variable is the extent to which it is only an index of other salient relationship concepts. Intuitively, one would suspect that variables such as sexual interaction, investment in the relationship, commitment, love, and others would all be highly correlated with the amount of time spent together. Time is needed to develop love and commitment, and love and commitment probably cause people to spend time together. Consequently, examination of this variable requires more specific study in order to determine its utility in understanding relationship development.

Sexual involvement. Other dyadic variables that refer to specific activities of couples have also been examined as predictors of relationship continuance. The impact of sexual involvement on the stability of premarital relationships has been debated over the years. Current studies do not provide a clear answer to this question.

Hill et al. (1976) found that whether or not a couple had had intercourse did not predict relationship stability; however, Simpson (1987) found that sexual intercourse increased the likelihood that couples would stay together over time, even when other salient relationship variables were controlled. Femlee et al. (1990) used a two-item measure asking how sexually intimate the couple was and how much they had invested in sex. This measure also differentiated stable and unstable couples (stable couples had higher scores on sexual involvement), but was not a unique predictor when compared with other variables. Of course, sexual involvement may also function as a marker or a result of other related concepts such as commitment, love, and amount of time spent together.

Communication behaviors. Several longitudinal studies have examined the effect of communication behaviors on relationship stability. Specifically, studies have examined communication as indexed by maintenance behaviors and self-disclosure. Maintenance behaviors have been conceptualized essentially as self-disclosures plus the extent to which individuals modify their own behaviors to benefit their relationships (Braiker & Kelley, 1979) or engage in nonintercourse physical affection (Surra & Longstreth, 1990). Self-disclosure may facilitate relationship development through its direct rewardingness, which should lead to positive feelings, and its ability to instill trust between partners (Sprecher, 1987).

Empirically, self-disclosure appears to be a significant predictor of relationship stability, although it has not been compared with other variables as a unique predictor. Berg and McQuinn (1986) found that for men, increased levels of self-disclosure to a partner were related to greater relationship stability. Similar results were reported by Hendrick et al. (1988), although separate analyses were not performed by gender. Sprecher (1987) distinguished between self-disclosure given to a partner versus disclosure perceived to be received from a partner. This study examined stability over a 4-year period of a sample of 48 couples. The higher the initial total couple self-disclosure, the more likely couples were to be together after 4 years. More significantly, the most important type of disclosure was the amount that men *perceived* that their partners disclosed to them, in comparison to what the man gave, the woman gave, or what the woman perceived she got.

Similar results were found when using maintenance behaviors as predictors of stability. Berg and McQuinn (1986) and Femlee et al. (1990) found that as single predictors, maintenance behaviors were positively related to relationship continuance. This finding was strengthened by the Surra and Longstreth (1990) study, in which a more immediate assessment of activities by couples showed that for men the number of maintenance behaviors engaged in with the partner differentiated intact from dissolved relationships.

Conflict. Several studies have examined conflict in developing premarital relationships, although the operationalization and measurement of conflict vary from study to study. Generally, global measures of initial conflict do not predict stability very adequately; however, studies that have examined conflict in specific areas, conflict resolution, stability of the conflict, and other aspects of conflict show promise.

Two studies (Berg & McQuinn, 1986; Femlee et al., 1990) operationalized conflict with a general scale developed by Braiker and Kelley (1979). This five-item scale assessed the frequency and seriousness of arguments, attempts to change the partner, and the expression of negative feelings. Conflict did not differentiate between continuing and noncontinuing premarital relationships.

Two recent studies have been more successful in identifying conflict-related factors that may predict stability. Lloyd (1990a) conducted a study that assessed conflict in 25 dating couples over a 2-week period and then contacted the couples 36 months later to see if they were still together. Conflict and conflict-related variables were assessed during the 2 weeks using daily diary records of interactions and disagreements with the partner. Those in continuing relationships reported lower persistence of the same problems over time than those in dissolved relationships. In addition, women in stable relationships reported more resolution of conflicts than did women in unstable relationships. Surra and Longstreth (1990) found that conflict concerning specific activities significantly predicted premarital breakup, but only for women. Stable relationships versus unstable ones were characterized by less conflict over sex, maintenance activities, partying, and companionship as perceived by the female partners. It appears then that these methods that assess conflict over time can identify factors that may lead to relationship instability.

Additionally, given the gender differences reported above, conflict may play a special role for women in premarital relationships. This suggestion would be consistent with previous work (Hill et al., 1976) that shows that women see relationship problems as more important in breakup than do men. The reason may be that women have more to lose in making a bad choice of a mate (e.g., economics, etc.) or are more interpersonally sensitive than men (Hill et al., 1976).

Dyadic Patterns

Similarity. The similarity of partners' individual attributes, attitudes, and preferences has been the major dyadic pattern examined as a predictor of premarital breakup. The inclusion of this variable as a predictor arises out of the previously discussed notion (see Chapter 3) that similarity is ostensibly indicative of compatibility in relationships and thus predictive of their stability.

Data from the Boston Couples Study (Hill et al., 1976) showed significantly higher similarity in the areas of involvement, age, academic achievement, educational aspirations, and physical attractiveness for stable versus unstable relationships. In contrast, Stephen (1984b) did not find that similarity of age and involvement predicted stability. He did find that the more individuals had constructed a shared system of meaning concerning intimate relationships ("symbolic interdependence"), the more likely they were to stay together.

When commitment, satisfaction, geographical proximity, similarity of involvement, and age were controlled, however, this measure of similarity was no longer predictive. Parks and Adelman (1983) found that a scale assessing individuals' perceptions of similarity in activities, attitudes, values, and outlook on life differentiated stable and unstable couples; however, similarity failed to be a unique predictor when compared with uncertainty concerning the partner.

More recently, Surra and Longstreth (1990) reported that similarity of preferences for activities predicted stability, but mainly for women. Women in stable relationships were more similar to partners in preferred activities related to food and errands, exercise, and sports and games than women in unstable relationships. Femlee et al. (1990) did find that similarity in race uniquely predicted breakup, when such variables as alternatives, length of relationship, underbenefiting, investment, and others were controlled. Those in biracial pairings were more likely to break up.

It appears that some types of similarity play a role in the stability of premarital relationships. Whether similarity's contribution to stability is unique is in question.

ஐ Social Network and Circumstantial Factors

Social network factors as predictors of premarital breakup have not been extensively studied. Only three studies have been performed that examine this issue; however, social network factors do show promise in informing us about relationship stability.

Lewis (1973b) was the first to examine network factors as predictors of relationship continuity. This study followed 316 individuals in dating relationships over a 10-week period. A six-item social reaction index was used to assess aspects of the participants' networks. This measure of social support asked participants to indicate the degree to which their own relatives and friends (a) included both partners in activities, and (b) perceived them as a "couple." People in stable pairings reported significantly higher support from their networks than those in unstable pairings.

Parks and Adelman's (1983) study expanded the study of network influences on relationship stability, by also assessing communication with the network. The social network factors examined included: (a) a measure of the degree to which the respondents generally communicated with their network members, as well as how often they had communicated with members during the past two weeks; and (b) the social reaction support measure by Lewis (1973b). Both of these network variables discriminated between stable and unstable couples, even when uncertainty about the partner was controlled. The more communication with and support from the network, the greater the stability of the relationships. These findings were supported by the Femlee et al. (1990) study, which showed that support from the partners' network was positively related to relationship continuance, even after controlling for such variables as alternatives, investments, length of relationship, and others.

The above findings were further elaborated in a study by Sprecher and Femlee (1991). This study followed 122 participants over 2 years and ascertained the ability of several social network variables to predict stability. Results showed that support from the females' networks was the best unique predictor of relationship continuance. Further analyses revealed that approval by the females' own family and friends were the specific types of support that best predicted stability. It thus appears that social network support, especially to female partners, may be important relative to other variables in facilitating stability in relationships.

Very little work has been done in identifying circumstantial factors that promote stability in relationships. Interestingly, the Stephen (1984a) study showed that being geographically separated was predictive of higher relationship stability, suggesting that there may be something unique about the relationships of these couples (e.g., more trust, commitment, etc.). On the other hand, separations may provide the opportunity to break off relationships. Hill et al. (1976) found that external factors related to separations (end of school, graduation, etc.) were the occasions when many relationship break ups occurred. The reader may consult Surra (1990) for a thorough discussion of external factors that may influence the choice of a mate.

❧ Conclusions

This chapter shows that some factors at all levels of the interpersonal process model are predictive of premarital relationship continuance. Not surprisingly, increased levels of love, commitment, investments into the relationship, satisfaction, communication behaviors, similarity, social network support, and others predicted relationship stability. Few of these factors clearly exhibited unique ability as predictors, however, when compared with each other. This is due to the difficulty in conceptualizing and independently measuring these constructs. Consequently, these aspects are related and likely measure some underlying construct, probably "relationship quality." If this is the case, not surprisingly "relationship quality" is a very good predictor of premarital stability. On the other hand, some variables show promise as unique predictors.

Commitment is one factor that may play a unique role in the stability of premarital relationships. Our review shows that such factors as love and comparison level for alternatives share common features with commitment to a relationship and these factors also are related to relationship continuity. These findings inform our understanding of how commitment operates to promote stability. Positive factors in the form of attraction to the relationship (love), as well as negative factors such as structural barriers (comparison level for alternatives) are likely involved in inducing commitment.

The frequency of interaction in premarital relationships also may play a unique role in courtship stability over time. Interaction frequency was a significant predictor even when comparison level for alternatives, investments, and other salient dyadic variables were compared; however, at present we have no studies that examine the extent to which interaction frequency is only a marker for the amount of love and commitment in the relationship. More systematic study will need to ferret out the specific sub-processes involved in relationship interaction.

Although not extensively studied, social network influences in the mate-selection process show promise as unique predictors of courtship stability. Network support, especially that given to female partners, predicted relationship continuity. These findings are congruent with the assumptions of the interpersonal process model that portray relationships as responsive to external influences. Future work in this area will need to explore the interactional processes by which networks promote relationship stability.

It is easy to take a romanticized view of courtship that focuses on commitment, love, communication, and other factors related to intimacy in relationships. A more realistic view has to acknowledge the negative aspects that can occur in premarital relationships. The following chapter reviews the empirical research on the darker side of courtship.

5

Courtships in Crisis

Thus far we have focused on the positive side of courtship—what brings partners together, what leads to progression in courtship, and who is likely to eventually marry. A thorough examination of courtship must include, however, a discussion of the "dark side" of courtship. Why are some premarital relationships "unsuccessful," either in the sense of breaking apart or in terms of containing highly negative interaction such as physical violence? We now turn to an examination of the process of breakdown and dissolution of courtships, followed by a discussion of physical violence and sexual aggression during courtship.

❧ Breakdown and Dissolution

Premarital relationships have long been viewed as a period of testing compatibility for eventual marriage. As partners assess their abilities to communicate, negotiate their differences and the similarities of their value systems, it is highly likely that some dyads will decide that the relationship is incompatible and therefore should be dissolved. What factors predict the eventual dissolution of a particular relationship? What leads to relationship breakdown and deterioration? How do premarital partners communicate their desire to withdraw from the partner? What events precipitate a breakup? This section will address these questions, turning first to a look at the antecedents of premarital breakup, followed by an examination of the process of breakdown and dissolution.

The Antecedents of a Broken Courtship

Early studies of premarital breakup concentrated on predicting over time which relationships would remain intact and which relationships would break apart. All of the studies reported in this section utilized a longitudinal design, wherein assessments taken at one point in the relationship were used to predict a breakup at a later point in time.

Burgess and Wallin (1953) conducted one of the first prospective studies of relationship breakup. Their classic study of 1,000 engaged couples demonstrated that broken engagements could be predicted by parental disapproval of the engagement, differences in leisure-time preferences, differences in religious faith, lower levels of affectional expression, and less confidence in the happiness of the future marriage.

Hill et al. (1976) prospectively studied 231 premarital couples over a period of 2 years. They found that couples who eventually broke apart (as compared to couples who remained together) were characterized at the beginning of the study by lower levels of love, unequal level of involvement between the partners, discrepant age and educational aspirations, differences in intelligence and physical attractiveness, a tendency to date less exclusively and shorter length of relationship. Other researchers have found lower satisfaction, involvement, commitment, love, maintenance, communication, rewards, investment, support from family and friends, length of relationship and hours spent together, and higher ambivalence, uncertainty, stability of conflict issues and alternative partners to be characteristic of premarital relationships that subsequently terminate (Berg & McQuinn, 1986; Femlee et al., 1990; Lloyd, 1990a; Lloyd et al., 1984; Rusbult, 1983; Simpson, 1987; Sprecher, 1987; Stephen, 1984b) (see Chapter 4 for a thorough discussion).

Overall, then, the antecedents of premarital relationship termination can be classified roughly into three categories: social incompatibility (such as discrepancy in educational aspirations), low relationship quality (such as low levels of love and communication) and social network influence (such as parental disapproval). Given that relationship termination can be predicted rather well from the nature and quality of the premarital relationship, the question then becomes at what point does the future of the relationship become apparent? We will use Surra's (1990) framework of early determinism versus gradual differentiation to give a two-part answer to this question.

Early determinism emphasizes that the demise of premarital relationships can be predicted quite early in the course of the relationship. Berg and McQuinn (1986) studied couples who had dated for a very short period of time (an average of only five dates), and found that levels of love, maintenance, comparison level, alternatives, and self-disclosure at this early stage of development were predictive of relationship continuation versus discontinuation 4 months later. Loyer-Carlson and Walker (1989), in an examination of the relationship-oriented reasons for the breakup of casual dating relationships, found that breakups that happened "quickly" (i.e., within 3 months) were attributed to interpersonal issues such as the lack of quality in the relationship and the poor interpersonal fit between the partners. Ultimately, "future viability" may be apparent very early in a relationship; the ability of partners to communicate comfortably as well as early attraction and love may be the means by which members of the dyad assess their compatibility at the earliest stages (Loyer-Carlson & Walker, 1989).

The gradual differentiation model argues, on the other hand, that relationships progress through periods of both growth/deterioration, openness/closedness, and stability/instability throughout their histories (Altman, Vinsel, & Brown, 1981; Surra, 1990). This model

proposes that there are multiple pathways to relationship development and dissolution as well as a variety of causes of change in relationships (Surra, 1990). Under the gradual differentiation model,
future termination would be apparent early on in only a subset of
relationships, and different factors would be hypothesized to affect
relationship termination in different relationships. Thus due to different developmental trajectories and interpersonal process, in some
relationships a breakup could be predicted in the first few weeks of
interaction, whereas in others a breakup could not be predicted until
several years of dating had gone by. We have highlighted Baxter's
work and our own work on the gradual differentiation model in the
next section of the chapter.

The Process of Relationship Breakdown and Dissolution

The gradual differentiation model has at its core an emphasis on
the process of relationship dissolution (Surra, 1990). Examining relationship breakdown and dissolution as processes necessitates a focus
on the internal workings and dynamics of the relationship (Baxter,
1986a). Process-oriented scholars study the factors that lead to relationship deterioration, the strategies partners use to convey that they
wish to terminate the relationship, and the different pathways or
trajectories characteristic of the dissolution process.

Relationship deterioration. Declines in satisfaction, uncertainty about
the future and destructive interaction patterns can lead to relationship breakdown (Duck, 1981). What leads to declines in relationship
satisfaction? Cross-sectional studies of courtship give us some information on the correlates of dissatisfaction. Dissatisfaction with
the relationship has been shown to be related to low level of rewards
(Cate et al., 1982), a lack of fairness in the distribution of rewards
(Walster, Walster, & Traupmann, 1978); a lack of investment in the relationship (Rusbult, 1983), destructive problem-solving techniques
(Rusbult, Johnson, & Morrow, 1986), and difficulty in resolving
conflict (Lloyd, 1987).

What leads to uncertainty about the future of the relationship?
Parks and Adelman (1983) reported that partners are more likely to

report uncertainty about the relationship when they report less communication with the partner, less communication with the partner's social network, and low levels of network support for the relationship. Planalp and Honeycutt (1985) examined the events that increase uncertainty. They found that competing relationships, betraying a confidence, a change in personality and values, and deception all contributed to increased uncertainty in relationships. In more than 50% of the cases such events decreased the closeness and intimacy of the relationship. A negative outcome was especially likely if the emotional impact of the event was negative, and if beliefs about the partner were strongly challenged.

Deception, the avoidance of relationship talk, and conflict are three types of premarital interaction that may lead to relationship deterioration. Deception is message distortion through misrepresentation or omission of information (Miller, Mongeau & Sleight, 1986). Unfortunately, the more intimate the relationship, the longer the duration of the relationship, and the more trust that partners have built up, the less accurate partners are in detecting deception (McCornack & Parks, 1990). The reasons for deceptive communication are varied, including an attempt to avoid hurting the partner, protecting one's self-image, and avoiding relationship trauma, conflict, or stress (Metts, 1989). When the reason for deception is to avoid hurting the partner, relationship satisfaction and closeness are less likely to be affected (Metts, 1989).

The topics of deception vary as well. The most common was *competing relationships*; this issue was likely to be concealed or distorted during stages of casual and serious dating, when partners are negotiating autonomy and togetherness. *Outside-relationship activities* was an issue of deception during engagement; partners may attempt to maintain their autonomy by failing to disclose or covering up the activities engaged in without the partner. Deception over the *state of the relationship* was most common in casual dating, and deception over *avoiding or decreasing contact* was most common in initial and casual dating (Tolhuizen, 1991).

An interesting form of "deception through omission" has been captured by Baxter and Wilmot (1985) in their study of "taboo" topics in close relationships. They identified six such topics: the state of the relationship, extra-relationship activity, relationship norms, prior relationships, conflict-inducing topics, and negative self-disclosure. Relationship talk was seen as something to be avoided, especially in situations where the partners were in the process of redefining their interaction; such talk was characterized as potentially destructive, risky, and ineffective. Most of the taboo topics were relationship-oriented in some way; talk concerning extra-relationship activity was avoided because of its implications for commitment, conflict was avoided because of the potential for incompatibility, and talk of norms was avoided because of the potential to cause redefinition of relational dynamics. It is indeed interesting that so many aspects of the relationship itself were considered "taboo" topics for discussion. Rather than attempting to understand the internal workings and definition of their relationship, partners appear to be highly prone to avoiding relationship examination. In a relationship already troubled by doubts or ambivalences the avoidance of relationship talk may eventually lead to deterioration.

What fuels the process of deterioration in relationships? Difficulties in communication may contribute to decline. Baxter and Wilmot (1983) found that partners in low-growth relationships (which included both relationships that had "stalled" and relationships that were declining) described their interaction as less satisfying, less important, less effective, and less personal than did partners in high-growth relationships. The process of decline is not merely a matter of the reversal of the growth of the relationship, however. Baxter (1983) noted that as a relationship declines, partners cannot "forget" all their knowledge of one another, and thus cannot reverse the process of "knowing" the other. Thus characteristics such as the ability to predict the thoughts and behavior of the partner as well as the ability to communicate through a variety of channels do not decline as the relationship deteriorates. Characteristics such as the smoothness and ease of communication and the personalness of self-disclosure do decline with deterioration of the relationship.

Conflict may also contribute to the process of deterioration in premarital relationships, albeit in a different manner for males versus females (Lloyd, 1987). For both males and females greater frequency of conflict is associated with greater relationship distress. Yet males and females may approach conflict from quite different perspectives. For females the key issue contributing to relationship decline appears to be difficulty in resolving conflicts, particularly those conflicts that the female has initiated herself. For males, on the other hand, the key issue is the stability of the conflict issue (that is, how often the same issue has come up in the past); conflict issues that are repeatedly brought up by the partner are particularly distressing. Thus the female partner's "pursuit of resolution" may initiate a cycle of relationship decline if the male partner perceives that the couple is "rehashing the same old issue" (Lloyd, 1987).

Lloyd and Cate (1985a) have described the attributions that partners give in retrospect for the deterioration of their relationships. While the relationship is growing (and moving toward deeper levels of commitment), partners overwhelmingly described dyadic factors as the key influences on relationships (Lloyd & Cate, 1985a; Surra, 1987). As the process of decline began and partners moved into a period of uncertainty about the future of the relationship, however, there was a shift in the nature of attributions for relationship change. Now partners described more individual and circumstantial reasons. Individual reasons were particularly associated with rapid deterioration in commitment; such reasons included perceived changes in partner's personality, feeling tied down and wanting freedom, and feeling that the relationship has progressed too rapidly. Circumstantial (or external) reasons were particularly associated with moderate declines in commitment; such reasons included a job transfer, illness, end of the school term, and so on.

The "whys" and "hows" of relationship dissolution. What reasons do premarital partners give for breaking off their relationships? And how do people go about breaking the "bad news" to a partner that the relationship is over? The relationship problems that precipitate a breakup vary widely and may include boredom with the relationship, uneven commitment, arguments, pressure from parents, or geographic separation (Clark & Labeff, 1986; Hill et al., 1976). Cupach and Metts (1986) found that the most common problems in premarital relationships that had dissolved were rooted in an individual; there was a strong tendency to attribute problems to a trait, disposition, or action of either the partner or oneself. Another problem unique to premarital relationships was a change in the definition of the relationship; some breakups were attributed to a relationship that was developing too quickly or to an uncomfortable transition between relationship stages.

Baxter (1986b) has examined in detail the reasons that partners offer for breaking up a romantic relationship. The most common reason offered was autonomy, or the desire for greater independence, followed by a lack of commonality, a failure to listen and support the partner, a lack of openness, infidelity, physical separation, an absence of equity, and an absence of romance. Females were more likely than males to mention autonomy, lack of openness, and lack of equity, whereas males were more likely than females to mention lack of romance as the precipitating factor.

The strategies for breaking off a romance, that is, the ways in which partners deliver the bad news, vary along two dimensions: directness and other-orientation (Baxter, 1986a). Directness refers to the extent to which the desire to end the relationship is explicitly stated to the partner; some strategies are quite direct, whereas others involve an attempt to break off the pairing without stating that breaking up is the goal. Direct strategies include *fait accompli* (telling the partner that the relationship is over with no hope of repair or compromise), *state-of-relationship talk* (a statement of the desire to break up in the context of a conversation about relationship problems), *attribution conflict* (an intense argument that becomes the reason for the breakup of the relationship) and *negotiated farewell* (a clear, bilateral communication that formally ends the relationship). Indirect strategies include *withdrawal* (spending less time with the partner or avoiding contact), *pseudodeescalation* (one or both partners state that they want the relationship to be less close or intense), *cost-escalation* (increasing the costs of the relationship in the hopes that the partner will break things off), and *fading away* (both partners know that the relationship has ended but do not talk about it) (Baxter, 1986a).

Other-orientation refers to the degree to which the disengager attempts to avoid hurting the partner in the process of breaking up; state-of-relationship talk, pseudodeescalation, fading away, and negotiated farewell are other-oriented, whereas cost-escalation, fait accompli, withdrawal, and attribution conflict are self-oriented (Baxter, 1986a). The type of strategy used in breaking up does vary by some characteristics of the relationship. The closer the relationship prior to the breakup, the greater the use of direct and other-oriented strategies. Direct strategies are also likely to be used when the partners desire contact in the future, the breakup is mutual, and the factor that precipitated the breakup is external to the relationship (Baxter, 1986a).

Trajectories of relationship dissolution. Inherent in the gradual differentiation and interpersonal process models is the idea that relationships take different pathways or trajectories as they develop and decline (Surra, 1990). We now present the result of two process studies of relationship dissolution that identify such trajectories. The model developed by Baxter (1984) highlights the process features of dissolution, whereas the model developed by Lloyd (1983) highlights the various pathways of both development and decline in premarital relationships.

Baxter (1984) first identified six "critical features" of the dissolution process: gradual versus sudden onset, unilateral versus bilateral desire to end the relationship, direct versus indirect termination strategy, rapid versus protracted negotiation over dissolution, presence versus absence of attempts to reconcile, and continuation versus termination of the relationship. While all possible combinations of these six critical features would yield over a hundred different relationship trajectories, Baxter finds eight types of dissolution trajectories to be most common. The most frequent trajectory was *preserving indirectness*—a unilateral decision to terminate the relationship, use of an indirect dissolution strategy that was resisted by the partner, with no attempts at reconciliation. *Ambivalent indirectness* involved a unilateral decision and an indirect dissolution strategy, followed by attempts at reconciliation and multiple disengagement attempts before final termination. *Mutual ambivalence* was almost identical to ambivalent indirectness, except that the desire to end the relationship was mutual. *Swift explicit mutuality* was characterized by bilateral desire to end the relationship, a direct approach, and swift termination. *Swift implicit mutuality* was similar with the exception of the use of an indirect approach. *Swift indirectness* involved a unilateral and indirect approach and resulted in the termination of the relationship on the first attempt. Both *ambivalent directness* and *swift directness* involved unilateral decisions and direct strategies. Ambivalent directness was further characterized by efforts to reconcile whereas swift directness involved a rapid termination without attempts at repair.

Baxter's (1984) trajectories emphasize the various pathways that people take as they end a romantic relationship. Another way to look at dissolution is to examine the types of *relationships* that dissolve. We have described broken relationships, using the retrospective graphing technique described in Chapter 4. (Details of the interview and extended results of this study appear in Lloyd, 1983.) We interviewed 100 premarital partners who had recently gone through the breakup of a serious romantic relationship. Each interviewee systematically described the entire development of the relationship, from the first date to the final goodbye, using the chance-of-marriage graph. These graphs were then clustered into five types of dissolved relationships.

Accelerated relationships both developed and deteriorated quite rapidly. Within 3 months of the first date the partners were committed, and, on average, reported an 88% chance of marriage. There were few downturns or negative events as the relationship was developing. Apparently one or two negative turning points sent the relationship into a tailspin, leading to a sharp deceleration of the relationship and a rapid dissolution phase. The following is a synopsis of one participant's description of his accelerated relationship (Lloyd, 1983):

> I met Mary on a raft trip in October. At that time, I was engaged to another girl. I broke off my engagement so I could get involved with Mary. At first our relationship was more physical than anything else—it really drew us together. Once we got physically accustomed to each other, we got closer mentally as well. I was really seeing a lot I liked about her—she fit my "ideal image." I felt like things could really work out well for us.

> In January she had feelings of uncertainty and uncomfortableness with everything around her—I think lots of things external to the relationship, and more so things within her, impacted on the relationship. On February 1st she said she didn't love me any more—she wanted to change the relationship to just friends. (pp. 47-48)

This anecdote illustrates rapidity of involvement and decline as well as the lack of negative turning points or conflict. In their entirety, accelerated relationships lasted 10 months on the average.

Low-level relationships were also relatively short, lasting on average 13 months from beginning to good-bye. These relationships were remarkably different from accelerated relationships in terms of their more gradual development (on average, partners dated 5 months before reaching the committed stage) and in terms of their lower chance of marriage (47%) at the point of greatest involvement. Low-level relationships contained few ups and downs; once a negative turning point occurred the relationship broke apart rather quickly (Lloyd, 1983):

> We got to know one another because of a relationship she was involved in with someone else. I became involved in that because I knew both Jean and her partner. Jean and I continued to talk about her relationship and about other things for several months—we had more and more talks and more and more visits. In February she terminated her other involvement—this was really the beginning of our involvement—we began to spend more time together. Jean and I began to build our lives around each other—she and I counted on the other to be there.
>
> In April, I said I wasn't able to give her the time and the part of myself that she wanted—she was reaching out for me, and I ran away from it. I'm 19, and I felt I needed to experience more things. (p. 48)

This relationship developed and ended rather suddenly. Although the interviewee expressed high behavioral involvement, on his graph the highest chance of marriage reached was only 45%.

Moderate relationships were the most symmetrical of the five types, both developing and dissolving at a moderate and even rate. On the average, these relationships reached 74% chance of marriage; partners in moderate relationships dated for approximately 6 months before reaching the committed stage and dated for 7 months in the committed stage before becoming uncertain about the future of the relationship. These relationships had a gradual dissolution phase that might best be characterized as a "fade out," with two or three negative turning points during dissolution. The following anecdote (Lloyd, 1983) illustrates this gradual disengagement:

> We had been seeing each other every weekend, and calling each other every day. However, around January, he began doing things with his friends more on the weekends. I knew something was wrong—Bob wasn't as open. I didn't say anything for several months about it, but eventually I initiated talking to him about what was happening. I asked Bob if it was another person — he said "no, but let's talk." I found out that back in January he'd been talking with a friend who said "I think Sue needs to get married." Bob had decided that we needed to deal with that—he told me he never wanted to marry anyone (but if he ever had wanted to marry, it would have been me). At this time I told him that I could live with that, that I was willing to continue the relationship without that kind of commitment, and when I began to feel uncomfortable with that, I'd let him know.
>
> In May, we had a disagreement—he thought I'd been sending him mixed messages—stating I didn't need a commitment but continuing on with the relationship just like before. We ended the relationship at this point. (p. 51)

On the average, moderate relationships lasted 17 months from first date to final termination.

Prolonged-turbulent relationships were the most up-and-down of the five types. These relationships lasted on average 31 months; partners dated for approximately 8 months before reaching the committed stage and spent an average of 14 months as a committed pair. The highest chance of marriage during the committed stage was 87%. Partners in prolonged-turbulent relationships noted a protracted period of ambivalence, spending 8 months in a state of uncertainty about the future of the relationship. These relationships contained an average of five major downturns; in many cases these downturns were temporary breakups with the partner. The following anecdote (Lloyd, 1983) begins after the couple have been going out for 2 years:

> Tom was going out with someone else—but he wouldn't tell me about it—I'd find out about it later. I finally got fed up with it and broke off

the relationship. A few days later we talked everything out—he told me he'd made a lot of mistakes, and he wanted to get back together. At this time he gave me a promise ring.

For the next three months, we got along really good. We spent the night together a lot—that brought us closer together. However, once I went back to school, I started feeling really tied down. I didn't feel like Tom was treating me like he should—he just didn't make me happy—he wasn't honest with me all the time. We broke up again over Christmas break.

Tom was really upset about the breakup—he was sorry, and he realized his mistakes—he wanted a second chance. I finally said okay, let's get back together. Things went really well for a couple of months—we looked at engagement rings, and talked about marriage.

The whole thing [breakup] happened during Spring break. His parents were gone—that was good—we could be alone, and anyway I didn't get along with his parents or friends at all. I found out he'd been smoking pot for five months, and I didn't like it. His friends were a bad influence on him, he had become money oriented . . . all these things began to pile up—we had lots of arguments—the whole week we didn't get along. I ended it—he wasn't in favor. (p. 53)

Prolonged-smooth relationships were the most enduring of the five types, lasting on average 54 months. These relationships attained the highest chance of marriage (92%) and were remarkable in their relative absence of negative turning points. Partners in prolonged-smooth relationships dated 16 months on average before reaching the committed stage and then spent an average of 28 months as a committed pair. The dissolution phase of these relationships was quite gradual, with a 7-month period of uncertainty about the future of the relationship. The following anecdote (Lloyd, 1983) illustrates such gradual unbonding. It begins after the couple had been going out for 5.5 years. During that time there had been no downturns in the relationship, and the chance of marriage had remained constant at 98% for 4 years:

Ever since November, I had been questioning whether I could marry Jim—I felt more like his sister than his "lover." It was a time when we had to make a decision about marriage—should we make it public, buy a ring? I had been questioning all along.

In August, when we went home to Missouri for a vacation, I met a guy—talked to him a lot. I realized through this that Jim and I had communication problems—I'd always thought before that men just didn't talk on a deep level. I realized also that such communication was important to me.

The final breakup occurred about two months later. I had actually made my decision in August, and I talked to him in October for the first time about it. I had not told Jim I had been questioning, so when I talked to him about it, I'd already made up my mind. Jim couldn't have changed it. (p. 55).

The five types of broken relationships—accelerated, low-level, moderate, prolonged-turbulent, and prolonged-smooth—were different in their levels of love and conflict. Partners in low-level relationships retrospectively reported the least love, especially in the earliest stages of the relationship. Generally, partners in prolonged-smooth and accelerated relationships reported the highest love. As the relationships came to a close, respondents with prolonged-turbulent relationships reported the lowest levels of love. None of the five types of relationships was characterized by a complete "lack of love," however; although the relationship was ending, respondents still reported feelings of attachment for their partners.

Conflict did not vary among the types during the stage of casual dating. During the committed stage, accelerated relationships were the lowest in conflict and prolonged-turbulent were the highest in conflict. During the dissolution phase, all five types were characterized by increased levels of conflict, with prolonged-turbulent relationships being highest in conflict once again (Lloyd, 1983).

These five types of dissolved relationships are quite interesting when compared to Cate's typology of courtships described in Chapter 3. The accelerated, intermediate, and prolonged patterns of relationship development appeared in both the sample of courtships that led to marriage and in the courtships that eventually broke apart. Indeed, the similarity between the two typologies is striking and leads us to speculate that some of the broken courtships could have led to marriage had it not been for the occurrence of a key negative turning point. Conversely, some of the courtships that resulted in marriage could easily have been broken apart by the occurrence of a negative turning point. Ultimately, courtships are affected in important ways not only by the quality of the interaction between the two partners, but also by timing and external forces. In some cases, mere chance is the factor that stands between marriage and a broken romance.

✎ Physical Violence and Sexual Aggression in Courtship

Because courtship is particularly romanticized in our culture, the motives and actions of courting partners are often imbued with both nobility and purity. Although there are a few references to violence and sexual exploitation in courting relationships in historical and early family studies literature (see, e.g., Kanin, 1957; Pleck, 1987; Waller, 1937), little attention was given to the possibility of negative courtship interaction until the 1980s. It was not until the work of Makepeace (1981), Cate, Henton, Koval, Christopher and Lloyd (1982), Laner and Thompson (1982), Koss and Oros (1982), Russell (1984), and others that issues of physical violence and rape in courtship were brought to the forefront.

Work on the dark side of courtship exploded during the 1980s (Lloyd, 1991). Following the lead of marital violence and rape research, research documented the incidence and the intrapersonal, network, and dyadic correlates of violence and sexual aggression. In the remainder of this chapter we review the literature on violence and sexual aggression, using Surra's (1987) framework of individual, network, dyadic, and circumstantial factors to organize the research. We then present a theoretical model that highlights how the very nature of courtship contributes to violence and sexual exploitation.

Incidence of Physical Violence and Sexual Aggression

Physical violence in courtship is, according to Sugarman and Hotaling (1989), typically defined as "the use or threat of physical force or restraint carried out with the intent of causing pain or injury to another" (p. 4). In practice, violence is operationalized as the number of times in the past year that premarital partners have engaged in pushing, shoving, slapping, kicking, biting, hitting with fists, hitting, trying to hit with an object, beatings and threats/use of a weapon (e.g., Cate et al., 1982). Stets and Henderson (1991) conducted a study of the incidence of physical abuse in courtship using a nationally representative sample. They found that 30% of the sample reported using physical violence in a dating relationship during the past 12 months; 31% reported being the recipient of such aggression. Sugarman and Hotaling (1989) calculated the average lifetime incidence rate across 20 studies to be as follows: aggressors—33% of males and 39% of females; victims—33% of males and 36% of females. Typically, when threats or verbal aggression are included, overall incidence is higher; when high school students versus college students are studied, the incidence is lower among high schoolers.

Physical violence in courtship is largely reciprocal, that is both partners are engaging in violent behavior toward each other; however, the types of violence and the incidence of injuries are not evenly distributed across men and women; men are two to four times as likely to use the more severe forms of violence (e.g., beatings, use of a weapon) and women are three to four times as likely to report injuries resulting from the violence (Makepeace, 1983; Sugarman & Hotaling, 1989). The greater strength of men and the greater propensity of women to be injured means that women are more likely to be the victims of violence; indeed, when asked to identify victim and aggressor, both men and women are likely to say that the woman is the victim and the man is the aggressor (Sugarman & Hotaling, 1989).

Sexual aggression in dating relationships is typically defined as sexual interaction, from petting to oral-genital contact to intercourse, which is gained against one's will through use of physical force, threats of force, continual arguments/pressure, use of alcohol/drugs and/or position of authority (Koss, 1988). Incidence rates of sexual aggression vary with the definition used. Restricting the definition to that of acquaintance or date rape (intercourse with a dating partner that occurs in a situation of force or threat of force) yields lifetime incidence rates for women ranging from 15% to 28% (Garrett-Gooding & Senter, 1987; Kilpatrick, Best, Saunders & Vernon, 1988; Korman & Leslie, 1982; Lane & Gwartney-Gibbs, 1985; Muehlenhard & Linton, 1987). Expanding the definition to intercourse engaged in as a result of verbal pressure or misuse of authority and attempted intercourse that was accompanied by physical force or threats of force increases the lifetime incidence rate for women significantly.[1] Koss (1988), in a national sample of college women, found that 39% of women had experienced an actual rape, an attempted rape, or had been coerced into intercourse. Eighty-four percent of the time the assailant was known to the victim. The figures jump sharply again when all types of unwanted sexual interaction are taken into account; fully one half to three fourths of college women report experiencing some type of sexual aggression in a dating relationship (Burke, Stets & Pirog-Good, 1988; Garrett-Gooding & Senter, 1987; Kanin & Parcell, 1977; Koss, 1988; Muehlenhard & Linton, 1987).

Sexual victimization is often accompanied by physical violence. In a representative survey of female victims of crime, injuries were reported in three fourths of the acquaintance rape situations, including bruises, black eyes, cuts, internal injuries, and unconsciousness (Belknap, 1989). Stets and Pirog-Good (1989) also noted a high correlation between sexual aggression and physical violence against women in their sample of college students.

Individual Factors in Physical Violence and Sexual Aggression

Although hundreds of research studies have examined the role of individual-level factors in physical abuse in courtship, as yet no clear profile of abusers or victims has emerged. Some studies do find a significant relationship between sex-role orientation and the male perpetration of physical abuse in courtship; however, there is some debate as to whether the male perpetrator is high in femininity or masculinity (Bernard, Bernard, & Bernard, 1985; Burke et al., 1988). Similarly, self-esteem is an inconsistent risk marker for physical abuse (Sugarman & Hotaling, 1989); some researchers report that abusers and victims in physically aggressive relationships are low in self-esteem (Burke et al., 1988; Deal & Wampler, 1986; Emery, 1983), but others do not (Arias, Samios, & O'Leary, 1987; Follingstad, Rutledge, Polek, & McNeill-Hawkins, 1988). The evidence on life stress events (e.g., being fired from a job, financial problems and/or academic problems) is somewhat more consistent, with stress being related to an increased incidence of physical abuse in courtship (Makepeace, 1983, 1987; Marshall & Rose, 1987; Mason & Blankenship, 1987).

There is some support for the intergenerational transfer of violence hypothesis. Several studies report a relationship between premarital physical abuse and either experiencing child abuse or witnessing parental violence (Barnes, Greenwood, & Sommer, 1991; DeMaris, 1990; Follingstad et al., 1988; Gwartney-Gibbs, Stockard, & Bohmer, 1987; Malone, Tyree, & O'Leary, 1989; Marshall & Rose, 1987; Riggs, O'Leary, & Breslin, 1990). The literature, however, is by no means entirely consistent on this issue, as a number of authors have failed to support the intergenerational transmission hypothesis (e.g., DeMaris, 1990; Stets & Pirog-Good, 1987).

The literature on sexual abuse in courtship does provide a fairly clear profile of the male abuser. Sexually abusive males, as compared to nonabusive males, tend to hold traditional beliefs about women, view their dating relationships as adversarial, display hostility toward women, and believe in rape-supportive myths (Christopher, Londen, & Owens, 1991; Garrett-Gooding & Senter, 1987; Koss, 1988; Lottes, 1988; Lundberg-Love & Geffner, 1989; Muehlenhard & Linton, 1987). They also exhibit greater physiological arousal to rape scenarios, greater acceptance of physical violence, greater hostility toward women, and may use sex as a means of expressing anger or dominance (Burkhart & Stanton, 1988; Malamuth, 1981; Stets & Pirog-Good, 1989). Sexually aggressive men are not characterized by a lack of sexual outlets; rather, they are "hypersexual." They are quite sexually active, reporting greater numbers of sexual partners, more quest for sexual experience, and the use of more exploitative techniques in their pursuit of sex than their nonaggressive peers (Kanin, 1985; Koss, Leonard, Beezley & Oros, 1985).

Female victims of sexual abuse in courtship differ very little from female nonvictims, however. There are no differences in self-esteem or other attitudinal or personality factors including assertiveness, feminist ideology, or belief in rape-supportive myths (Ageton, 1988; Amick & Calhoun, 1987; Korman & Leslie, 1982; Koss & Dinero, 1989). Recent studies on sexual aggression in dating relationships have documented a link for females between child sexual abuse and later sexual victimization in a dating relationship (Koss & Dinero, 1989; Lundberg-Love & Geffner, 1989). Lundberg-Love and Geffner (1989) explain this relationship in terms of a lowered ability to resist sexual aggression. The victim of childhood sexual abuse may discount her feelings of danger in a situation of sexual aggression for fear that she is overreacting; as the aggression proceeds, she may become paralyzed as the situation reenacts her childhood trauma. Koss and Dinero (1989) hypothesize that childhood sexual abuse serves as a vulnerability factor, contributing to negative self-identity and adult sexual attitudes and activities that may place her at risk.

Ultimately, individual factors are at best poor predictors of who will be the perpetrators and victims of physical violence and who will be victimized by sexual aggression. Why are intrapersonal variables such poor predictors of involvement in courtship violence? We offer three reasons. First, as noted in the chapters on theories of mate selection, intraindividual factors are often accorded more weight than is warranted by empirical support due to our historical emphasis on intrapsychic phenomena that has grown out of the psychoanalytic, personality, and medical model traditions. As the interpersonal process models of courtship demonstrate, however, dyadic factors are more predictive of future state of a relationship than are individual personality and traits. Second, to date, the studies of courtship violence have almost exclusively utilized relatively homogeneous populations (i.e., college students) who may not vary a great deal on the variables of interest (e.g., life stress); study of more representative samples might indeed yield results that are more in keeping with the marital violence literature. Third, perhaps violence and sexual aggression are so widespread that nearly everyone either has experienced them or will experience them at some point in the future. This means that rather than focusing on the presence versus absence of violence, we may need to examine different "types" of violent relationships (Lloyd, 1990b). The pathbreaking work of Follingstad et al. (1988) demonstrates that women who have experienced one isolated incident of violence are not different from women who have never experienced violence; however, women who have experienced multiple acts of violence are clearly differentiated from these two groups. Future work that emphasizes the different "types" of violent relationships may indeed find clearer risk markers for ongoing violence in courtship.

Network Factors in Physical Violence and Sexual Aggression

Most abuse, whether physical violence or sexual aggression, occurs in a private situation (Laner, 1983; Makepeace, 1981; Roscoe & Benaske, 1985). When physical violence does occur in front of witnesses, intervention is likely to occur in less than 50% of the incidents. Men more than women are likely to report third-party intervention in violent behavior (Laner, 1983). Thus social networks are unlikely to have an influence on a particular occurrence of violence or sexual aggression.

Networks do play a key role in the norms surrounding violence and sexual exploitation because networks may either support the legitimacy of such aggression or emphasize the inappropriateness of such behavior. DeKeseredy (1988) developed a model of abuse in dating relationships that highlights the role of male peer support; his study of 333 male undergraduates demonstrated that male network support may influence both the initiation and maintenance of sexual and physical abuse of female dating partners, particularly under conditions of high stress. Gwartney-Gibbs et al. (1987) found support for this relationship as well; they further demonstrated that females who have experienced sexual aggression in a dating relationship are likely to have female friends who have been victimized as well.

Gwartney-Gibbs and Stockard (1989) conducted a particularly interesting study of the role of networks in sexual aggression. They identified three distinct peer group types: a nonaggressive peer group (the respondent did not have any male friends who had been aggressors or female friends who had been victims), a female victimization peer group (respondent had female friends who had been sexually victimized but had no sexually aggressive male friends), and a sexually aggressive peer group (had both sexually aggressive male friends and sexually victimized female friends). Differences by peer group revealed that females with sexually aggressive peer groups were much more likely to have been victimized than females with the other two types of peer groups. Males with a sexually aggressive peer group were significantly more likely to have been physically violent in a dating relationship. The groups also differed in living arrangements, alcohol use, and educational aspirations. Males who had nonaggressive peers groups were the most likely to live at home and the least likely to use alcohol heavily, whereas males with an aggressive peer group were most likely to live in a fraternity and view the social aspects of college as highly important. Females who had a female-victimized peer group were the most career and school oriented.

Gwartney-Gibbs and Stockard (1989) concluded that the sexual aggressiveness of males in one's peer group is an important factor in predicting whether females in the peer group have been victimized as well. They noted the virtual absence of the fourth possible peer group type, that of a network composed of sexually aggressive males and nonvictimized females. Ultimately, the male peer group may serve to legitimize male dominance and sexual conquest (Kanin, 1957; 1985).

Dyadic Factors in Physical Violence and Sexual Aggression

The dyadic factors associated with physical violence in courtship can be broken into three categories: precipitators, dynamics, and relationship correlates. What seems to precipitate physical abuse and sexual aggression in courtship? Emotion-related precipitators of physical and sexual abuse include jealousy, anger and frustration, and sexual denial (Emery, Lloyd, & Castleton, 1989; Laner, 1983; Makepeace, 1981; Stets & Pirog-Good, 1987). In a detailed assessment of the precipitating causes of violence, Laner (1983) identified nine categories of factors. In order from most frequently mentioned to least frequently mentioned, the precipitators were: *emotions* (jealousy, guilt, insecurity), *problem-solving dilemmas* (misunderstandings and arguments), *temperament* (angry, irritated), *reflexive factors* (feeling deceived, attacked, or insulted), *misjudgment* (teasing or fooling around that turned serious), *personality* (stubborn, selfish, inconsiderate), *rejection* (breaking up, loss of interest in relationship), *power struggles* (dependency/dominance, role definitions, sexual denial) and *alcohol/drugs*. Women listed temperament and power struggles as precipitating factors more often than did men, whereas men listed emotions, reflexive factors, and rejection more often than women.

What are the dynamics of the aggressive situation in courtship? Henton, Cate, Koval, Lloyd, and Christopher (1983) asked both victims and perpetrators to give their perceptions of the violent act. Perpetrators were most likely to interpret their violence as confusion, followed by anger, love, fear, and sadness. Less than 3% of the aggressors interpreted their violence as a sign of hate. Victims interpreted the violence directed at them in similar ways, mentioning anger, confusion, love, and fear. The attribution of love may be indicative of the romantic veneer that surrounds relationships in general and courtship in particular (Henton et al., 1983; Lloyd, 1991).

How do victims react to the occurrence of violence and sexual aggression in their relationships? Henton et al. (1983) asked those involved in violence to indicate their feelings and behavioral reactions to the most recent incident of violence. More than 50% of the victims indicated feeling angry and hurt; behaviorally they responded by talking to the partner, fighting back, crying, leaving the scene, and moving out of reach. Most of the aggressors indicated they felt sorry or hurt after the incident; they responded by apologizing, trying to make up, and talking to the partner.

In a sexually aggressive situation victims were the most likely to use reasoning in their attempts to resist the aggression; when the aggression includes rape or attempted rape, the victim is also highly likely to have used physical struggle or force as a resistance technique (Belknap, 1989; Koss, 1988). In addition, victims report screaming and attempting to leave the scene as responses (Belknap, 1989). Ironically, a well-known perpetrator (e.g., someone the victim has a long-term relationship with) is more likely to complete a rape and to injure the victim than is an acquaintance (Belknap, 1989).

Looking at longer-term impact of the violence, we find that most of the couples involved in a violent incident report either that the violence had no impact on their relationship or that the violence actually improved things. Only about one fourth to one third indicate that the violence made their relationship worse; similarly, only a few respondents indicate that the violence caused their relationship to terminate (Cate et al., 1982; O'Keefe, Brockopp, & Chew, 1986).

The length and commitment level of the relationship have been correlated with physical and sexual abuse in courtship. Physical abuse is more likely to occur once relationships have reached the serious stage or cohabitation; the risk of physical abuse increases with the length of the relationship (Aizenman & Kelley, 1988; Arias et al., 1987; Stets & Pirog-Good, 1990). Similarly, sexual aggression is more likely to occur in long-term versus casual relationships; rape in particular is likely to occur at the hands of a well-known assailant rather than an acquaintance (Belknap, 1989; Burke et al., 1988; Kanin, 1957).

What are the relationship characteristics associated with physical violence in courtship? Partners in physically abusive courtships exhibit more negative affect, conflict, verbal aggression, ambivalence about continuing the relationship, indirect styles of negotiation (i.e., withdrawal or crying), confrontation, blaming the partner, and expressing anger (Billingham & Sack, 1987; Bird, Stith, & Schladale, 1991; Lloyd, Koval, & Cate, 1989). Partners in abusive courtships are also distinguished by their use of persistence as a negotiation strategy, high investment in the relationship, and the belief that the partner can be changed (Lloyd et al., 1989).

Ironically, partners involved in violent courtships do not seem to love each other less than those involved in nonviolent relationships (Arias et al., 1987; Follingstad et al., 1988; Gryl, Stith & Bird, 1991), nor do they seem to be highly dissatisfied with their relationships (O'Leary et al., 1989). Follingstad et al. (1988) did find a difference in love between one-time and ongoing abused women; the women experiencing ongoing abuse report greater love and commitment for their partners.

Interaction patterns/relationship issues are related to sexual abuse as well. In a study of successful versus unsuccessful resisters to rape, Amick and Calhoun (1987) found that unsuccessful resisters were in more isolated situations, in a steady relationship with the aggressor, and had sex with the aggressor in the past. Miscommunication about sexuality is also cited as a risk factor for sexual aggression. Males tend to view females' behavior as more "sexual" than do females, which may result in the misinterpretation of petting as a signal that the female desires intercourse. The result is that males may feel that "she led me on," and that they have a right to impose their will in situations wherein mixed signals are being received (Muehlenhard, 1988; Muehlenhard & Linton, 1987). The traditional sexual script dictates that men be the initiators and that women indicate their willingness to engage in intercourse in an indirect manner; this script fosters the view that a woman's resistance is only token and can be ignored (Check & Malamuth, 1983; Muehlenhard, 1988).

While both males and females report using physical violence in courtship, their motivations for the use of violence as a means of control seem to differ. Men may use physical violence to maintain their control over their partners and get their own way or as a tactic of intimidation and "striking fear" into the partner. Women, on the other hand, may resort to violence to keep the relationship intact, to gain some control over the abusive situation or in retaliation, self-defense, anger, and frustration (Emery et al., 1989; Lloyd & Emery, 1990; Mason & Blankenship, 1987; Stets & Pirog-Good, 1990; Sugarman & Hotaling, 1989). Rape and sexual aggression are also acts viewed as resulting from the power imbalance that exists between men and women (Lundberg-Love & Geffner, 1989; Muehlenhard & Linton, 1987; Stets & Pirog-Good, 1989). Specifically, sexual aggression has been associated with male attempts to dominate, change, and impose one's will on the partner (Stets & Pirog-Good, 1989).

Circumstantial Correlates of Physical Violence
and Sexual Aggression

Alcohol use has been cited as a common feature of both physically violent and sexually aggressive episodes. Couples report that alcohol was an influence in 50% of cases of physical abuse (Bogel-Albritten & Albritten, 1985; Makepeace, 1981). Upwards of three fourths of sexually aggressive men and half of female victims report use of alcohol at the time of the incident (Koss, 1988; Lundberg-Love & Geffner, 1989; Muehlenhard & Linton, 1987). The use of alcohol may serve as a disinhibitor for the aggressor or as an excuse for the aggressive behavior. The victim's use of alcohol may decrease her ability to resist aggression; unfortunately, it also leads many to blame the victim for her own victimization (Lundberg-Love & Geffner, 1989).

Several situational components of the date itself are related to the likelihood of sexual aggression and physical violence. As mentioned earlier, aggression on a date is likely to occur in private. Makepeace (1981) noted that 51% of physically aggressive incidents occurred in a residence, 22% in vehicles, and 22% out-of-doors. If the man initiated the date, paid the expenses, and drove, sexual aggression was more likely to occur (Muehlenhard & Linton, 1987). If he pays for the date, there is an implied bargain of sex for money (Bailey, 1988); both high school-age and college-age men believe that sexual aggression is more justified under such circumstances (Lundberg-Love & Geffner, 1989). Going to the man's apartment is interpreted as a sign that the woman desires sex, and, indeed, both men and women reported more sexual aggression when in a man's physical domain (Koss, 1988; Muehlenhard, 1988; Muehlenhard & Linton, 1987).

A Conceptual Model of the Dark Side of Courtship

Lloyd (1991) recently proposed a conceptual model of the "dark side" of courtship. This model emphasizes how the very nature of courtship itself potentially contributes to the problems of physical violence and sexual aggression. Two facets of courtship in particular are hypothesized to increase the likelihood that violence and sexual aggression will occur. These factors are the different contexts of courtship for men versus women and the highly romanticized nature of courting relationships.

Courtship is currently pervaded with different "themes" for males versus females (Lloyd, 1991). For males the predominant theme is "staying in control," whereas for females the predominant theme is "dependence on the relationship." These themes are a result of socialization, media portrayals, and the stereotypic notions we hold about men and women. Women are the "lovers"—the persons in charge of the emotional maintenance of the relationship (Huston, in preparation), whereas men are the "leavers"—the persons in charge of regulating emotional distance/closeness (Lloyd, 1991). Ultimately women "need" relationships in a way that men do not; women need relationships as a sign of their emotional maturity and personal fulfillment (Breines & Gordon, 1983).

Lloyd (1991) hypothesized that these themes inadvertently contribute to the problems of violence and sexual exploitation. The male theme of control justifies his imposition of his will on the partner; it is his prerogative to demand compliance from his partner by whatever means necessary, even through violent or exploitative means. The theme of control also means that he is concerned with regulating commitment in the relationship; the use of aggression may be one means to maintain emotional distance or closeness in a close relationship (Mayseless, 1991). The female theme of dependence may constrain her to remain in a relationship that is violent or exploitative. Given that marriage and relationships are viewed as key components of female identity, the cultural ideology of "any man is better than no man" may cause her to accept aggression as part and parcel of courtship (Lloyd, 1991).

For both males and females courtship is surrounded by a romantic ideal. This romanticism includes the idea that love conquers all, that love can solve any problem, and that all the negative aspects of courtship will go away as soon as marriage takes place (Waller, 1951). The impact of this romantic view is clearly evident in the work of Henton et al. (1983). Romanticism allows violent behavior to be downplayed because violence is attributed to situational factors (such as anger) and not to a fundamental problem in the relationship or partner. Henton et al. (1983) clearly demonstrate that both victims and aggressors strive to overlook, ignore, or reframe the aggressive behavior; the fact that more than 50% of those experiencing a violent incident indicated that the violence either had no effect or improved their relationship is testimony to the power of romance in courtship. Romanticism ultimately serves as a constraining factor, encouraging couples to stay together despite extremely negative interaction.

The Impact of Violence and
Sexual Aggression in Courtship

What is the impact of abuse in courtship? On a short-term basis, studies of physical abuse report that reactions vary from emotions such as anger and hurt feelings to responding with physical abuse itself (Henton et al., 1983; Emery et al., 1989). Reactions to sexual aggression and rape include anger, fear (specifically, fear of being alone), sexual distress, and depression (Kilpatrick et al., 1988).

Research has also revealed long-term effects of courtship abuse. In interviews with women who had been in physically abusive dating relationships, Emery et al. (1989) found that attitudes toward men and relationships had changed. These women were wary of partners who tried to control them, had a "check list" of characteristics to avoid in potential partners, and were reluctant to trust males again. In an interesting contradiction, women reported either having developed stronger self-concepts as a result of dealing with the abuse or harboring feelings of "cheapness" and embarrassment along with low self-concepts. In a study of the long-term impact of rape by a date, Kilpatrick et al. (1988) noted symptoms of major depression, social phobia, and sexual dysfunction.

Finally, there is concern that the use of physical violence and sexual aggression in courtship will continue into marriage. Early studies of marital abuse confirm that abuse may have begun premaritally (Gayford, 1975). The fact that some support exists for the generational transmission of abuse (Bernard & Bernard, 1983; Emery, 1983; Follingstad et al., 1988) plus findings that experiencing dating violence may be associated with more accepting attitudes of marital and dating violence (Cate et al., 1982; Deal & Wampler, 1986; Emery, 1983) lead to the conclusion that the experience of abuse in courtship may predispose individuals to inflict or sustain such behavior in marital relationships as well. Recent longitudinal work by O'Leary et al. (1989) clearly confirms the carryover of abuse in courtship to the marriage.

‎ Conclusions

Courtship, although imbued with purity and nobility, clearly has a "dark side." The negative aspects of courtship range from deception and deterioration to physical violence and sexual exploitation. Such negativity does not always herald the demise of the relationship, however. Both Kelly et al. (1985) and O'Leary et al. (1989) demonstrated the potentially destructive impact on marriage of negative interaction patterns established during courtship. Premarital partners would do well to pay close attention to the warning signs that are inherent in negative courtship interaction.

‌ Note

1. The figures for the sexual victimization of men in dating relationships are considerably lower, especially intercourse that is accompanied by force or threats of force (Lane & Gwartney-Gibbs, 1985). As a result of the low incidence of victimization of men, sexual aggression is conceptualized primarily as a problem of male aggression and female victimization. For further information on unwanted sexual activity reported by men, see Muehlenhard and Cook (1988).

6

Future Perspectives on Courtship

This final chapter has two purposes. First, we will discuss some research related theoretical and methodological issues that need to be addressed in the future. Second, we will suggest some changes that might be expected in the institution of courtship in the coming years.

⊷ Research and Theory Needs

The picture of the processes that lead to marriage that has been painted in this book is far from clear, yet significant advances in research have taken place. A clear improvement has been made in the methodologies used in studying developing relationships. Most significant is the trend toward longitudinal studies, virtually all of which have been completed since 1970. These longitudinal studies allow for a better understanding of the causal factors that operate in the movement to marriage. In addition, there appears to be a trend away from looking at courtship as a discrete series of stages toward a stance of viewing courtship from an interactional perspective. This interactional perspective assumes that relationships evolve not only due to various static individual and relationship properties, but also by what transpires in the interaction of couples (e.g., communication, conflict, etc.). Much additional theoretical and empirical work is needed, however, to help us better understand the courtship processes.

The first step in improving courtship research is the development of theories or conceptual frameworks to explain the movement to marriage. Social exchange theory and its related theories of investment and equity have shed some light on mate-selection in recent years. Yet there is a need for theories or models that more directly assess the *development* of premarital relationships. In Surra's (1990) excellent review of courtship research, she has suggested that present research implies four different models of relationship development toward marriage:

1. gradual differentiation
2. early determinism
3. incremental convergence and divergence
4. progressive stages

Further theoretical development and empirical work with these models will require that attention be paid to certain methodological and conceptual issues. In addition, courtship research has largely ignored the area of social cognition.

Gradual differentiation. The gradual differentiation model (briefly described in Chapter 3) is essentially synonymous with what we previously called the "interpersonal process model" and the close relationships model developed by Kelley et al. (1983). These models assume that relationships move to marriage along different trajectories, although common patterns can be identified. The model also assumes that relationships over time exhibit both growth and deterioration, that causation between variables is reciprocal, that relationship properties emerge over time, and that the pathways are influenced by variables at different levels of analysis (individual, dyadic, interaction, social networks, etc.). These assumptions require that certain methodological and conceptual issues be considered. First, any model that posits change over time must be tested with longitudinal designs. In the case of this model, such longitudinal designs must assess the variables of interest at numerous time points in the development of the relationship, so that cycles of growth and deterioration can be detected. Longitudinal studies can also be suggestive of the direction of causality between variables.

Second, tests of this model will require assessment of variables at several levels of analysis. For example, at the individual level, little attention has been given to the role of individual dispositions in the courtship process. For example, no longitudinal studies of premarital stability have examined such factors as perspective-taking (Davis & Oathout, 1987; Long & Andrews, 1990) and private self-consciousness (Franzoi, Davis, & Young, 1985), both of which have been shown to predict interpersonal behavior in premarital relationships. In addition, other dispositional variables might show promise in helping explain movement to marriage. Negative affect, a dispositional characteristic (Watson & Clark, 1984), may have an impact on various relationship characteristics. Those low in negative affectivity have been shown to value social relationships and work hard to maintain those relationships, while those high in negative affectivity are more independent and tend to be loners (Watson & Clark, 1984).

Little research examines the characteristics of social networks as they affect the movement to marriage (for an exception, see Parks & Adelman, 1983, study discussed in Chapter 4). It seems plausible that network members may serve different purposes over time. Early in a relationship the approval or disapproval of a potential partner by network members may assist in determining the suitableness of that possible match. Leslie, Huston, and Johnson (1986) suggested that parents indirectly influence partner choice because individuals may deepen their involvement with only those who they know will be approved by parents. Other indirect influences may exist, such as partners gaining information about each other by using network members for social comparison and observation of the partners' interacting with their networks (Surra, 1990). Later, as relationships develop to more involved stages, positive and negative influence attempts by both parents and children increase (Leslie et al., 1986). Also, it may be that the addition of mutual friends over time to a couples' network could create obstacles from leaving the relationship because partners may see loss of these new friends as costly (Milardo, 1982). In support of the above, one retrospective study of courtship (Surra et al., 1988) has suggested that network factors are connected to both positive and negative changes in premarital relationships.

Circumstantial events may also contribute to declines and advances in courtship. Surra et al. (1988) found circumstantial factors in a retrospective study to be related mainly to downturns in courtships.

Early determinism. The early determinism model (Surra, 1990) outcomes discussed earlier in this book (stability, satisfaction) assumes that relationship development is largely determined by early characteristics of the relationship such as social exchange variables and other relationship factors. Supposedly, these factors operate similarly for all couples. Although this model might imply that longitudinal methods could err on the side of collecting data only in the early phases of relationships, such an assumption ignores the possibility that some identified early factor may exert its influence through factors or processes that occur later in the relationship. Thus attention to only early factors or processes may portray an incomplete scenario of the relationship-development process.

Theory development with the early determinism model needs to be expanded to include concepts at more than the relationship level of analysis (Surra, 1990). Again the individual disposition of negative affectivity may have implications for initial couple interaction. This personal disposition could obviously be important in affecting those variables identified as early determinants of relationship stability, such as maintenance behaviors, love, and self-disclosure (Berg & McQuinn, 1986). Those high on negative affectivity are less gregarious and less pleasant to be around than those low on this disposition (Watson & Clark, 1984), thus potentially affecting one's ability to initiate and maintain new relationships. Additionally, network factors, especially family network factors, may operate in the initial choice of a dating partner, as cited in the above study by Leslie et al.

(1986); however, such network factors need much more study. Further, little work has examined the circumstantial factors that may enhance or deter the development of relationships toward marriage. For example, do circumstantial factors play a role in the type of person that we meet? Kerckhoff (1974) persuasively argued that social context can limit the field of desirable marriage partners. At present, some cross-sectional work has found that the size and heterogeneity of the population from which people choose mates is related to whom people choose to affiliate (e.g., Surra, 1990). Similarly, it seems likely that social context initially communicates something about potential partners that would be used in the choice of a potential mate and maintenance of a relationship. For example, meeting a person at a fundamentalist Christian event implies certain values and behavioral tendencies that might be quite divergent from those of someone who was encountered at an X-rated movie, which obviously has implications for choice of a mate.

Incremental convergence and divergence. The incremental convergence and divergence model posits that the progression of changes in relationship states and outcomes is similar for all couples, with relationship properties emerging over time due to the interaction of couples (Surra, 1990). Again, in order to detect changing states and outcomes, along with emerging properties over time, frequent longitudinal data collection points must be incorporated into designs that test this model. Also, convergence and divergence is seen to come about mainly due to communication (Surra, 1990). Consequently, this model views relationship change from a fairly narrow perspective. Our argument has been that change is due to factors at various levels of analysis, not just the interactional level of this model. Other possible causal factors and relationship outcomes need to be further explored. For example, convergence and divergence in levels of structural commitment over time may occur, with changes being influenced by people's perceptions of alternatives to the present relationship. The symmetry of relational involvement, a factor shown to predict stability in premarital relationships (Hill et al., 1976), might arise due to separate influences in each partner's social network or due to such personal dispositions as adult attachment styles (Hazan

& Shaver, 1987), which supposedly influence the degree to which people feel comfortable in deepening their relationships with romantic partners.

Progressive stages. Progressive stage models (see discussion of various stage models in Chapter 4) portray change and causes of change in relationship states as occurring similarly for all couples in a series of set stages. Relationship properties are seen as existing early in relationships but also emerging over time. The causes of change are seen to occur at several levels of analysis, although little attention has been paid to circumstantial, external causes (Surra, 1990). Future research will have to address this shortcoming. Probably the greatest weakness of these models is the lack of specificity as to what defines a "stage." Sequential models define stages by examining the ability of some factor (attitude similarity, personality complementarity, etc.) at some previous time point to predict a future relationship state, such as breakup or degree of movement toward marriage. In other words, to uncover a previous stage, one must observe some future event such as relationship breakup. Future researchers could make stronger arguments for the existence of stage models by demonstrating qualitative or quantitative changes throughout the course of a relationship. The identification of qualitative change would require that research show differing interrelationships over time between salient courtship variables. A case for the existence of stage models from a quantitative perspective would require that this quantitative change be either discontinuous in nature (e.g., make sudden shifts) or, in the case of gradual change, a phenomenological redefinition of the relationship. As with other models, changes indicative of progressive stages require that data be collected frequently over time.

Social cognition. Little attention has been paid to cognitive processes that may operate in the mate-selection process. This is interesting, given that many of the past models of courtship development assume that rational decisions are made concerning the selection of a mate (Cate & Lloyd, 1988). Much of the current thinking in the area of close relationships posits that there are important processes that mediate between behavior and satisfaction with relationships (e.g., Bradbury & Fincham, 1989). This perspective holds that one partner's behavior is processed by the other partner through attention, perception, interpretation, and the production of affect. This processing stage is affected by the: (a) proximal context, which includes recent thoughts and feelings prompted by external events, previous interaction with the partner, etc.; and (b) the distal context, which includes rather stable and enduring characteristics such as individual attributes of partners, general relationship expectations, relationship characteristics that have emerged through the history of interaction with the partner, etc. Satisfaction with the relationship emerges from these processes. This perspective proposes that appraisal of the partner and relationship between interactions is an important part of the distal context. This area is ripe for the development and testing of theoretical propositions relative to relationship development (see Bradbury & Fincham, 1989, and Huston & Rempel, 1989, for a fuller discussion). The authors are currently conducting research that examines the role of "relationship thinking" between interactions in premarital relationships. Relationship thinking predicts satisfaction with individuals' behavioral interactions with their partners and the amount of self-disclosure in those interactions (Cate, 1991). Similarly, in relation to the processing stage of this framework, Fletcher and Fitness (1990) found that positive thinking that occurs during actual interaction is a predictor of dyadic satisfaction in premarital relationships. These recent studies illustrate the need to incorporate a social cognitive perspective in theory development in courtship.

❧ The Future of Courtship

We thought it appropriate to close this volume with some speculation on the "future" of courtship. As noted at the end of Chapter 2, there are several themes of change and continuity in the history of American courtship. Changes were seen in who had control over the activities of courtship, in the nature and rates of premarital sexual interaction, in the extent of community/parental control over courtship activities, in the openness of communication and the definition of love, and in the age at first marriage. Continuity remained in the relative autonomy accorded young people in their choice of mates, the importance of love (however currently defined) to future marital happiness, and in the fact that the "one and only" was likely to be encountered at the same point in time that both culture and individual defined as the "right time to marry!"

Despite the long-term emphasis on the importance of love to relationships and a remarkable tendency for pair relationships to survive as the primary "family" form, most predictions about the future of courtship and marriage in the popular literature are rather dire. At the beginning of the decade of the 1990s, however, it seems clear that courtship and marriage will survive through the beginning of the next millennium.

The major trends of the last half of the twentieth century may presage the direction of courtship in the future. The age at first marriage may continue to rise, although it will eventually be capped around age 30 for those desiring children by the age-related declines in female fertility. Just as medical advances profoundly affected family relationships in the twentieth century (through reliable control over procreation, increased likelihood of infant survival beyond the first year, and extension of the life span), however, medical advances in the area of fertility are likely to continue to affect courtship and marriage. The increasing possibility of conception and successful pregnancy at age 40 and beyond may help push the age at first marriage back even further; and the possibility of gestation outside the female body may increase the equality of the sexes (particularly when gestation inside the male body becomes a reality).

Medical advances are also likely to continue to affect premarital sexuality. An emphasis on monogamous sexual relationships and non-promiscuous sexual practices has risen over the past decade largely due to the rise in AIDS and other sexually transmitted diseases (Megli & Morgan, 1991). Just as the birth control pill revolutionized sexuality in the late 1960s, however, it may be that a cure for AIDS and reliable methods for the prevention of transmission of the virus will signal yet another wave of liberalism in sexual interaction. Whether this future liberalism will include more emphasis on "open" marriage and courtships as well as a decrease in sexual jealousy (as predicted by Murstein in his 1984 essay on the future of mate selection) remains to be seen.

Cohabitation is likely to become an ever more common stage in the process of courtship. Recently the popular literature has emphasized the importance of learning how to "get relationships right" the first time (Megli & Morgan, 1991). Cohabitation may take on increasing importance as the time to "test the marital waters" and assess marital compatibility. Concomitantly, as the age at marriage continues to increase, cohabitation may become the preferred form for premarital pair bonding among those who are beyond the early adult years.

The twentieth-century movement toward greater equality between the sexes will likely have a profound impact on courtship and marriage in the future (Murstein, 1984). As women become equal players in the marketplace (both in terms of wages and level of career advancement), relationships between men and women at home cannot remain unaffected. The activities of courtship may eventually become equally initiated and planned by either partner: "popping the question" and buying an engagement ring may fall under female as well as male purview. The marriage gradient (i.e., the tendency for males to marry down and females to marry up) should disappear, or, particularly in terms of age, reverse (Murstein, 1984).

Time for relationships, time to meet the perfect mate, and time for courtship are likely to be major themes of the future. Prusank et al. (1991) noted that popular literature of the 1980s emphasized time as a problem for the modern couple. Ironically, time was also the solution to the problem: scheduling quality time with one's mate was often the main advice for relationship maintenance and repair. The recent advent of dating services and video matchmaking clearly reflect our preoccupation with finding the right mate quickly and efficiently. The initial events of courtship thus may be changing from informal introductions by one's friends to formal services that may maximize the chances of compatibility.

Finally, courtship has increasingly become a life stage that individuals go through more than one time. Today more than 40% of marriages involve remarriage of one or both of the partners (Coleman & Ganong, 1990). If divorce and remarriage rates continue at current levels, then "courtship the second time around" may eventually entail unique rituals and patterns of interaction. For example, when one or both courting partners have children, their courtship activities may increasingly involve interaction with the children and may eventually result in an emphasis on "testing compatibility" of the future parent-child as well as husband-wife relationships.

Ultimately, unlike many futurists in the popular literature, we do not predict the eventual decline of courtship and marriage. As Murstein (1984) noted, the "couple" has remained remarkably stable as the basic unit of American society. We believe that the "couple" will remain a primary unit, and that love, togetherness, quality time, good communication, and mutually satisfying sexuality will remain important themes in our culture through the next century.

References

Adams, C. R. (1946). The prediction of adjustment in marriage. *Educational and Psychological Measurement, 6,* 185-193.

Ageton, S. S. (1988). Vulnerability to sexual assault. In A. W. Burgess (Ed.), *Rape and sexual assault II,* (pp. 221-244). New York: Garland Press.

Aizenman, M., & Kelley, G. (1988). The incidence of violence and acquaintance rape in dating relationships among college men and women. *Journal of College Student Development, 29,* 305-311.

Altman, I., Vinsel, A., & Brown, B. B. (1981). Dialectic conceptions in social psychology: An application to social penetration and privacy regulation. In L. Berkowitz (Ed.), *Advances in experimental social psychology: Vol. 14.* (pp. 1-40). New York: Academic Press.

Amick, A. E., & Calhoun, K. S. (1987). Resistance to sexual aggression: Personality, attitudinal and situational factors. *Archives of Sexual Behavior, 16,* 153-163.

Antill, J. K. (1983). Sex role complementarity versus similarity in married couples. *Journal of Personality and Social Psychology, 45,* 145-155.

Arias, I., Samios, M., & O'Leary, K. D. (1987). Prevalence and correlates of physical aggression in courtship. *Journal of Interpersonal Violence, 2,* 82-90.

Austin, W. G. (1974). *Studies in "equity with the world": A new application of equity theory.* Unpublished doctoral dissertation, University of Wisconsin, Madison.

Bailey, B. L. (1988). *From front porch to backseat: Courtship in twentieth century America.* Baltimore: The Johns Hopkins University Press.

Barnes, G. E., Greenwood, L., & Sommer, R. (1991). Courtship violence in a Canadian sample of male college students. *Family Relations, 40,* 37-44.

Baxter, L. A. (1983). Relationship disengagement: An examination of the reversal hypothesis. *The Western Journal of Speech Communication, 47,* 85-98.

Baxter, L. A. (1984). Trajectories of relationship disengagement. *Journal of Social and Personal Relationships, 1,* 29-48.

Baxter, L. A. (1986a). Accomplishing relationship disengagement. In S. Duck & D. Perlman (Eds.), *Understanding personal relationships* (pp. 243-265). London: Sage.

Baxter, L. A. (1986b). Gender differences in the heterosexual relationship rules embedded in breakup accounts. *Journal of Social and Personal Relationships, 3,* 289-306.

Baxter, L. A., & Wilmot, W. W. (1983). Communication characteristics of relationships with differential growth rates. *Communication Monographs, 50,* 264-272.

Baxter, L. A., & Wilmot, W. W. (1985). Taboo topics in close relationships. *Journal of Social and Personal Relationships, 2,* 253-269.

Belknap, J. (1989). The sexual victimization of unmarried women by non-relative acquaintances. In M. Pirog-Good & J. Stets (Eds.), *Violence in dating relationships* (pp. 205-218). New York: Praeger.

Bell, R. R., & Coughey, K. (1980). Premarital sexual experience among college females, 1958, 1968 and 1978. *Family Relations, 29,* 353-357.

Bentler, P. M., & Newcomb, M. D. (1978). Longitudinal study of marital success and failure. *Journal of Consulting and Clinical Psychology, 46,* 1053-1070.

Berg, J. H., & McQuinn, R. D. (1986). Attraction and exchange in continuing and noncontinuing dating relationships. *Journal of Personality and Social Psychology, 50,* 942-952.

Bernard, J. L., Bernard, S. L., & Bernard, N. L. (1985). Courtship violence and sex-typing. *Family Relations, 34,* 573-576.

Bernard, M. L., & Bernard, J. L. (1983). Violent intimacy: The family as a model of love relationships. *Family Relations, 32,* 283-286.

Berscheid, E., Dion, K., Walster, E., & Walster, G. W. (1971). Physical attractiveness and dating choice: A test of the matching hypothesis. *Journal of Experimental Social Psychology, 7,* 173-189.

Berscheid, E., Snyder, M., & Omoto, A. M. (1989). The relationship closeness inventory: Assessing the closeness of interpersonal relationships. *Journal of Personality and Social Psychology, 57,* 792-807.

Berscheid, E., & Walster, E. (1974a). A little bit about love. In T. Huston (Ed.), *Foundations of interpersonal attraction* (pp. 355-381). New York: Academic Press.

Berscheid, E., & Walster, E. (1974b). Physical attractiveness. *Advances in Experimental Social Psychology, 7,* 158-216.

Billingham, R. E., & Sack, A. R. (1987). Conflict tactics and the level of emotional commitment among unmarrieds. *Human Relations, 40,* 59-74.

Bird, G. W., Stith, S., & Schladale, J. (1991). Psychological resources, coping strategies, and negotiation styles as discriminators of violence in dating relationships. *Family Relations, 40,* 45-50.

Blumstein, P., & Kollock, P. (1988). Personal relationships. *Annual Review of Sociology, 14,* 467-490.

Bogel-Albritten, R. B., & Albritten, W. L. (1985). The hidden violence: Courtship violence among college students. *Journal of College Student Personnel, 19,* 201-204.

Bolton, C. D. (1961). Mate selection as the development of a relationship. *Marriage and Family Living, 23,* 234-240.

Booth, A., Brinkerhoff, D. B., & White, L. K. (1984). The impact of parental divorce on courtship. *Journal of Marriage and the Family, 46,* 85-94.

Booth, A., Johnson, D. R., White, L. K., & Edwards, J. N. (1987). Divorce and marital instability over the life course. *Journal of Family Issues, 7,* 421-442.

Bradbury, T. N., & Fincham, F. D. (1989). Behavior and satisfaction in marriage: Prospective mediating processes. In C. Hendrick (Ed.), *Close relationships* (pp. 119-143). Newbury Park, CA: Sage.

Braiker, H. B., & Kelley, H. H. (1979). Conflict in the development of close relationships. In R. L. Burgess & T. L. Huston (Eds.), *Social exchange in developing relationships* (pp. 135-168). New York: Academic Press.

Breines, W., & Gordon, L. (1983). The new scholarship on family violence. *Signs, 8,* 490-531.

Bumpass, L. L., & Sweet, J. A. (1972). Differentials in marital instability: 1970. *American Sociological Review, 37,* 754-766.

Burgess, E. W., & Cottrell, L. S. (1939). *Predicting success or failure in marriage.* New York: Prentice-Hall.

Burgess, E. W., & Wallin, P. W. (1953). *Engagement and marriage.* New York: Lippincott.

Burgess, E. W., & Wallin, P. W. (1954). *Courtship, engagement and marriage.* New York: Lippincott.

Burke, P. J., Stets, J. E., & Pirog-Good, M. A. (1988). Gender identity, self esteem and physical and sexual abuse in dating relationships. *Social Psychology Quarterly, 51,* 272-285.

Burkhart, B. R., & Stanton, A. L. (1988). Sexual aggression in acquaintance relationships. In G. W. Russell (Ed.), *Violence in intimate relationships* (pp. 43-65). New York: PMA.

Burr, W. R. (1973). *Theory construction and the sociology of the family.* New York: John Wiley.

Caplow, T., Bahr, H. M., Chadwick, B. A., Hill, R., & Williamson, M. H. (1982). *Middletown families: Fifty years of change and continuity.* Minneapolis: University of Minnesota Press.

Cate, R. M. (1991, May). *Relationship thinking: A measure and some initial studies.* Paper presented at the International Network Conference on Personal Relationships, Normal, IL.

Cate, R. M., Henton, J. M., Koval, J. E., Christopher, F. S., & Lloyd, S. A. (1982). Premarital abuse: A social psychological perspective. *Journal of Family Issues, 3,* 79-90.

Cate, R. M., Huston, T. L., & Nesselroade, J. R. (1986). Premarital relationships: Toward the identification of alternative pathways to marriage. *Journal of Social and Clinical Psychology, 4,* 3-22.

Cate, R. M., & Lloyd, S. A. (1988). Courtship. In S. Duck (Ed.), *Handbook of personal relationships* (pp. 409-427). New York: John Wiley.

Cate, R. M., Lloyd, S. A., & Henton, J. M. (1986). The effect of equity, equality and reward level on the stability of students' premarital relationships. *Journal of Social Psychology, 125,* 715-721.

Cate, R. M., Lloyd, S. A., Henton, J. M., & Larson, J. H. (1982). Fairness and reward level as predictors of relationship satisfaction. *Social Psychology Quarterly, 45,* 177-181.

Check, J. V., & Malamuth, N. M. (1983). Sex role stereotyping and reactions to depictions of stranger versus acquaintance rape. *Journal of Personality and Social Psychology, 45,* 344-356.

Cherlin, A. (1981). *Marriage, divorce, remarriage.* Cambridge, MA: Harvard University Press.

Christopher, F. S., Londen, H. L., & Owens, L. A. (1991, May). *Individual and relational correlates of premarital sexual aggression.* Paper presented at the International Network Conference on Personal Relationships, Normal, IL.

Clark, R. E., & Labeff, E. E. (1986). Ending intimate relationships: Strategies of breaking off. *Sociological Spectrum, 6,* 245-367.

Cohen, M. (1988). *The sisterhood.* New York: Simon & Schuster.

Coleman, M., & Ganong, L. H. (1990). Remarriage and stepfamily research in the 1980s: Increased interest in an old family form. *Journal of Marriage and the Family, 52,* 925-940.

Coontz, S. (1988). *The social origins of private life: A history of American families 1600-1900.* New York: Verso.

Cuber, J. F., & Harroff, P. B. (1966). *Sex and the significant Americans.* New York: Penguin.

Cupach, W. R., & Metts, S. (1986). Accounts of relational dissolution: A comparison of marital and nonmarital relationships. *Communication Monographs, 53,* 311-334.

Davis, M. H., & Oathout, H. A. (1987). Maintenance of satisfaction in romantic relationships: Empathy and relational competence. *Journal of Personality and Social Psychology, 53,* 397-410.

Deal, J. E., & Wampler, K. S. (1986). Dating violence: The primacy of previous experience. *Journal of Social and Personal Relationships, 3,* 457-471.

DeKeseredy, W. S. (1988). *Woman abuse in dating relationships: The role of male peer support.* Toronto: Canadian Scholars Press.

DeMaris, A. (1990). The dynamics of generational transfer in courtship violence: A biracial exploration. *Journal of Marriage and the Family, 52,* 219-231.

Demos, J. (1986). *Past, present and personal: The family and the life course in American history.* New York: Oxford University Press.

Duck, S. (1981). A topography of relationship disengagement and dissolution. In S. Duck (Ed.), *Personal relationships 4: Dissolving personal relationships* (pp. 1-30). New York: Academic Press.

Duck, S. W., & Sants, H.K.A. (1983). On the origin of the specious: Are personal relationships really interpersonal states? *Journal of Social and Clinical Psychology, 1,* 27-41.

Ehrmann, W. (1959). *Premarital dating behavior.* New York: Bantam.

Emery, B. C. (1983). *Factors contributing to violence in dating relationships.* Unpublished master's thesis, Oregon State University, Corvallis.

Emery, B. C., Lloyd, S. A., & Castleton, A. (1989). *Why women hit back: A feminist perspective.* Paper presented at National Council on Family Relations Annual Meeting, New Orleans, LA.

Farber, B. (1957). An index of marital integration. *Sociometry, 20,* 117-134.

Farber, B. (1964). *Family: Organization and interaction.* San Francisco: Chandler.

Fehr, B. (1988). Prototype analysis of the concepts of love and commitment. *Journal of Personality and Social Psychology, 55,* 557-579.

Femlee, D., Sprecher, S., & Bassin, E. (1990). The dissolution of intimate relationships: A hazard model. *Social Psychology Quarterly, 53,* 13-30.

Filsinger, E. E., & Thoma, S. J. (1988). Behavioral antecedents of relationship stability and adjustment: A five-year longitudinal study. *Journal of Marriage and the Family, 50,* 785-795.

Fletcher, G., & Fitness, J. (1990). Occurrent social cognition in close relationship interaction: The role of proximal and distal variables. *Journal of Personality and Social Psychology, 59,* 464-474.

Foa, U., & Foa, E. (1974). *Societal Structures of the Mind.* Springfield, IL: Charles C Thomas.

Follingstad, D., Rutledge, L. R., Polek, D. S., & McNeill-Hawkins, K. (1988). Factors associated with patterns of dating violence toward college women. *Journal of Family Violence, 3,* 169-182.

Fowers, B. J., & Olson, D. H. (1986). Predicting marital success with PRE-PARE: A predictive validity study. *Journal of Marriage and Family Therapy, 12,* 403-413.

Franzoi, S. L., Davis, M. H., & Young, R. D. (1985). The effects of private self-consciousness and perspective taking on satisfaction in close relationships. *Journal of Personality and Social Psychology, 48,* 1584-1594.

Friedan, B. (1963). *The feminine mystique.* New York: Dell.

Furstenberg, F. (1966). Industrialization and the American family: A look backward. *American Sociological Review, 31,* 326-337.

Gadlin, H. (1977). Private lives and public order: A critical view of the history of intimate relations in the United States. In G. Levinger & H. Raush (Eds.), *Close relationships: Perspectives on the meaning of intimacy* (pp. 33-72). Amherst: University of Massachusetts Press.

Garrett-Gooding, J., & Senter, R. (1987). Attitudes and acts of sexual aggression on a university campus. *Sociological Inquiry, 57,* 348-371.

Gayford, J. J. (1975). Wife battering: A preliminary survey of 1000 cases. *British Medical Journal, 1,* 79-90.

Glenn, N. D. (1990). Quantitative research on marital quality in the 1980's: A critical review. *Journal of Marriage and the Family, 52,* 818-831.

Glenn, N. D., & Coleman, M. (1988). *Family relations: A reader.* Belmont, CA: Wadsworth.

Glick, P. C. (1975). Some recent changes in American families. *Current Population Reports* (P-23, No. 52).

Glick, P. C. (1984). Marriage, divorce and living arrangements. *Journal of Family Issues, 5,* 7-26.

Gordon, M. (1981). Was Waller ever right? The rating and dating complex reconsidered. *Journal of Marriage and the Family, 43,* 67-76.

Greven, P. (1970). *Four generations: Population, land, and family in Colonial Andover, Massachusetts.* Ithaca, NY: Cornell University Press.

Gryl, F. E., Stith, S. M., & Bird, G. W. (1991). Close dating relationships among college students: Differences by use of violence and gender. *Journal of Social and Personal Relationships, 8,* 243-264.

Gwartney-Gibbs, P., & Stockard, J. (1989). Courtship aggression and mixed sex groups. In M. Pirog-Good & J. Stets (Eds.), *Violence in dating relationships* (pp. 185-204). New York: Praeger.

Gwartney-Gibbs, P., Stockard, J., & Bohmer, S. (1987). Learning courtship aggression: The influence of parents, peers and personal experiences. *Family Relations, 36,* 276-282.

Hamilton, G. V., & MacGowan, K. (1929). *What is wrong with marriage.* New York: Albert & Charles Boni.

Hanson, S. L., & Tuch, S. A. (1984). The determinants of marital instability: Some methodological issues. *Journal of Marriage and the Family, 46,* 631-642.

Hatfield, E., & Sprecher, S. (1986). Measuring passionate love in intimate relations. *Journal of Adolescence, 9,* 383-410.

Hazan, C., & Shaver, P. (1987). Romantic love conceptualized as an attachment process. *Journal of Personality and Social Psychology, 52,* 511-524.

Hendrick, C., & Hendrick, S. S. (1986). A theory and method of love. *Journal of Personality and Social Psychology, 50*, 392-402.

Hendrick, S. S. (1981). Self-disclosure and marital satisfaction. *Journal of Personality and Social Psychology, 40*, 1150-1159.

Hendrick, S. S., & Hendrick, C. (1992). *Romantic love.* Newbury Park, CA: Sage.

Hendrick, S. S., Hendrick, C., & Adler, N. L. (1988). Romantic relationships: Love, satisfaction, and staying together. *Journal of Personality and Social Psychology, 54*, 980-988.

Henton, J. M., Cate, R. M., Koval, J. E., Lloyd, S. A., & Christopher, F. S. (1983). Romance and violence in dating relationships. *Journal of Family Issues, 4*, 467-582.

Hill, C. T., Rubin, Z., & Peplau, L. A. (1976). Breakups before marriage: The end of 103 affairs. *Journal of Social Issues, 32*(1), 147-168.

Huston, T. L. (1973). Ambiguity of acceptance, social desirability, and dating choice. *Journal of Experimental Social Psychology, 9*, 32-42.

Huston, T. L. (In preparation). Premarital precursors of the psychological infrastructure of marriage. In R. Gilmour (Ed.), *Theoretical perspectives on personal relationships.* Hillsdale, NJ: Lawrence Erlbaum.

Huston, T. L., & Levinger, G. (1978). Interpersonal attraction and relationships. *Annual Review of Psychology, 29*, 115-156.

Huston, T. L., McHale, S. M., & Crouter, A. C. (1986). When the honeymoon's over: Changes in the marriage relationship over the first year. In S. Duck & R. Gilmour (Eds.), *The emerging field of personal relationships* (pp. 109-132). Hillsdale, NJ: Lawrence Erlbaum.

Huston, T. L., & Rempel, J. K. (1989). Interpersonal attitudes, dispositions, and behavior in family and other close relationships. *Journal of Family Psychology, 3*, 177-198.

Huston, T. L., & Robins, E. (1982). Conceptual and methodological issues in studying close relationships. *Journal of Marriage and the Family, 44*, 901-925.

Huston, T. L., Surra, C., Fitzgerald, N., & Cate, R. (1981). From courtship to marriage: Mate selection as an interpersonal process. In S. Duck & R. Gilmour (Eds.), *Personal relationships 2: Developing personal relationships* (pp. 53-88). London: Academic Press.

Johnson, D. J., & Rusbult, C. E. (1989). Resisting temptation: Devaluation of alternative partners as a means of maintaining commitment in close relationships. *Journal of Personality and Social Psychology, 57*, 967-980.

Johnson, M. P. (1973). Commitment: A conceptual structure and empirical application. *Sociological Quarterly, 4*, 359-406.

Johnson, M. P. (1985). *Commitment, cohesion, investment, barriers, alternatives, constraint: Why do people stay together when they really don't want to?* Paper presented at the Theory Construction and Research Methodology Workshop, National Council on Family Relations Annual Meeting, Dallas, TX.

Julien, D., Markman, H. J., & Lindahl, K. M. (1989). A comparison of a global and a microanalytic coding system: Implications for future trends in studying interactions. *Behavioral Assessment, 11*, 81-100.

Kanin, E. J. (1957). Male aggression in dating-courtship relations. *American Journal of Sociology, 10*, 197-204.

Kanin, E. J. (1985). Date rapists: Differential sexual socialization and relative deprivation. *Archives of Sexual Behavior, 14*, 219-231.

Kanin, E. J., & Parcell, S. R. (1977). Sexual aggression: A second look at the offended female. *Archives of Sexual Behavior, 6*, 67-76.

Kelley, H. H. (1983). Love and commitment. In H. H. Kelley, E. Berscheid, A. Christensen, J. H. Harvey, T. L. Huston, G. Levinger, E. McClintock, L. A. Peplau, & D. R. Peterson, *Close relationships* (pp. 265-314). New York: Freeman.

Kelley, H. H., Berscheid, E., Christensen, A., Harvey, J. H., Huston, T. L., Levinger, G., McClintock, E., Peplau, L. A., & Peterson, D. R. (1983). *Close relationships*. New York: Freeman.

Kelley, R. K. (1969). *Courtship, marriage and the family*. New York: Harcourt Brace.

Kelly, C., Huston, T. L., & Cate, R. M. (1985). Premarital relationship correlates of the erosion of satisfaction in marriage. *Journal of Social and Personal Relationships, 2*, 167-178.

Kelly, L. E., & Conley, J. J. (1987). Personality and compatibility: A prospective analysis of marital stability and marital satisfaction. *Journal of Personality and Social Psychology, 52*, 27-40.

Kerckhoff, A. C. (1974). The social context of interpersonal attraction. In T. L. Huston (Ed.), *Foundations of interpersonal attraction* (pp. 61-78). New York: Academic Press.

Kerckhoff, A. C., & Davis, K. E. (1962). Value consensus and need complementarity in mate selection. *American Sociological Review, 27*, 295-303.

Kidd, V. (1975). Happily ever after and other relationship styles: Advice on interpersonal relations in popular magazines, 1951-1973. *Quarterly Journal of Speech, 61*, 31-39.

Kilpatrick, D. G., Best, C. L., Saunders, B. E., & Vernon, L. J. (1988). Rape in marriage and dating relationships: How bad is it for mental health? *Annals of the New York Academy of Sciences, 528*, 335-344.

Kitson, G. C., Barbi, K. B., & Roach, M. J. (1985). Who divorces and why: A review. *Journal of Family Issues, 6*, 255-293.

Koller, M. R. (1951). Some changes in courtship behavior in three generations of Ohio women. *American Sociological Review, 16*, 366-370.

Korman, S. K., & Leslie, G. R. (1982). The relationship of feminist ideology and date expense sharing to perceptions of sexual aggression in dating. *Journal of Sex Research, 18*, 114-129.

Koss, M. P. (1988). Hidden rape: Sexual aggression and victimization in a national sample of students in higher education. In A. W. Burgess (Ed.), *Rape and sexual assault II* (pp. 3-25). New York: Garland Press.

Koss, M. P., & Dinero, T. E. (1989). Discriminant analysis of risk factors for sexual victimization among a sample of college women. *Family Relations, 57,* 242-250.

Koss, M. P., Leonard, K. E., Beezley, D. A., & Oros, C. J. (1985). Nonstranger sexual aggression: A discriminant analysis of the psychological characteristics of undetected offenders. *Sex Roles, 12,* 981-992.

Koss, M. P., & Oros, C. J. (1982). Sexual experiences survey: A research instrument investigating sexual aggression and victimization. *Journal of Consulting and Clinical Psychology, 50,* 455-457.

Kurdek, L. A. (1991). Marital stability and changes in marital quality in newly wed couples: A test of the contextual model. *Journal of Social and Personal Relationships, 8,* 27-48.

Lane, K. E., & Gwartney-Gibbs, P. A. (1985). Violence in the context of dating and sex. *Journal of Family Issues, 6,* 45-59.

Laner, M. R. (1983). Courtship abuse and aggression: Contextual aspects. *Sociological Spectrum, 3,.* 69-83.

Laner, M. R., & Thompson, J. (1982). Abuse and aggression in courting couples. *Deviant Behavior, 3,* 229-244.

Larsen, A. S., & Olson, D. H. (1988). Predicting marital satisfaction using PREPARE: A replication study. *Journal of Marital and Family Therapy, 15,* 311-322.

Lee, J. A. (1973). *The colors of love: An exploration of the ways of loving.* Don Mills, Ontario: New Press.

Leigh, G. K., Holman, T. B., & Burr, W. R. (1987). Some confusions and exclusions of the SVR theory of dyadic pairing: A response to Murstein. *Journal of Marriage and the Family, 49,* 933-937.

Leslie, L. A., Huston, T. L., & Johnson, M. P. (1986). Parental reactions to dating relationships: Do they really make a difference? *Journal of Marriage and the Family, 48,* 57-66.

Levinger, G., & Rands, M. (1985). Compatibility in marriage and other close relationships. In W. Ickes (Ed.), *Compatible and incompatible relationships* (pp. 309-331). New York: Springer Verlag.

Levinger, G., Rands, M., & Talaber, R. (1977). *The assessment of involvement and rewardingness in close and casual pair relationships* (National Science Foundation Technical Report DK). Amherst: University of Massachusetts.

Levinger, G., Senn, D. J., & Jorgensen, B. W. (1970). Progress toward permanence in courtship: A test of the Kerckhoff-Davis hypotheses. *Sociometry, 33,* 427-443.

Levinger, G., & Snoek, J. D. (1972). *Attraction in relationships: A new look at interpersonal attraction.* Morristown, NJ: General Learning.

Lewis, R. A. (1972). A developmental framework for the analysis of premarital dyadic formation. *Family Process, 11,* 17-48.

Lewis, R. A. (1973a). A longitudinal test of a developmental framework for premarital dyadic formation. *Journal of Marriage and the Family, 35,* 16-25.

Lewis, R. A. (1973b). Societal reaction and the formation of dyads. *Sociometry, 36,* 409-418.

Lewis, R. A., & Spanier, G. (1979). Theorizing about the quality and stability of marriage. In W. R. Burr, R. Hill, F. I. Nye, & I. L. Reiss (Eds.), *Contemporary theories about the family: Vol.I.* (pp. 268-294). New York: Free Press.

Lloyd, S. A. (1983). *A typological description of premarital relationship dissolution.* Unpublished doctoral dissertation, Oregon State University, Corvallis.

Lloyd, S. A. (1987). Conflict in premarital relationships: Differential perceptions of males and females. *Family Relations, 36,* 290-294.

Lloyd, S. A. (1990a). A behavioral self-report technique for assessing conflict in close relationships. *Journal of Social and Personal Relationships, 7,* 265-272.

Lloyd, S. A. (1990b). Asking the right questions about the future of marital violence research. In D. Besharov (Ed.), *Family violence: Research and public policy issues* (pp. 93-107). Washington DC: AEI Press.

Lloyd, S. A. (1991). The darkside of courtship. *Family Relations, 40,* 14-20.

Lloyd, S. A., & Cate, R. M. (1985a). Attributions associated with significant turning points in premarital relationship development and dissolution. *Journal of Social and Personal Relationships, 2,* 419-436.

Lloyd, S. A., & Cate, R. M. (1985b). The developmental course of conflict in premarital relationship dissolution. *Journal of Social and Personal Relationships, 2,* 179-194.

Lloyd, S. A., Cate, R. M., & Henton, J. M. (1984). Predicting premarital relationship stability: A methodological refinement. *Journal of Marriage and the Family, 46,* 71-76.

Lloyd, S. A., & Emery, B. C. (1990, November). *The dynamics of violence in courtship.* Paper presented at the National Council on Family Relations National Conference, Seattle, WA.

Lloyd, S. A., Koval, J. E., & Cate, R. M. (1989). Conflict and violence in dating relationships. In M. Pirog-Good & J. Stets (Eds.), *Violence in dating relationships* (pp. 126-144). New York: Praeger.

Locke, H. J. (1951). *Predicting adjustment in marriage.* New York: Holt, Rinehart & Winston.

Locke, H. J., & Wallace, K. M. (1959). Short marital-adjustment and prediction tests: Their reliability and validity. *Marriage and Family Living, 21,* 251-255.

Long, E., & Andrews, D. (1990). Perspective taking as a predictor of marital adjustment. *Journal of Personality and Social Psychology, 59,* 126-131.

Lottes, I. L. (1988). Sexual socialization and attitudes toward rape. In A. W. Burgess (Ed.), *Rape and sexual assault II* (pp. 193-219). New York: Garland.

Loyer-Carlson, V., & Walker, A. J. (1989, November). *Causal attributions and the dissolution of casual-dating relationships*. Paper presented at National Council on Family Relations Annual Meeting, New Orleans, LA.

Lujansky, H., & Mikula, G. (1983). Can equity theory explain the quality and stability of romantic relationships? *British Journal of Social Psychology, 22,* 101-112.

Lund, M. (1985). The development of investment and commitment scales for predicting continuity of personal relationships. *Journal of Social and Personal Relationships, 2,* 3-23.

Lundberg, F., & Farnham, M. (1947). *Modern woman: The lost sex.* New York: Harper and Brothers.

Lundberg-Love, P., & Geffner, R. (1989). Date rape: Prevalence, risk factors and a proposed model. In M. Pirog-Good & J. Stets (Eds.), *Violence in dating relationships* (pp. 169-184). New York: Praeger.

Lynd, R. S., & Lynd, H. M. (1929). *Middletown: A study in contemporary American culture.* New York: Harcourt, Brace & Company.

Lynd, R. S., & Lynd, H. M. (1937). *Middletown in transition: A study in cultural conflicts.* New York: Harcourt, Brace & Company.

Lystra, K. (1989). *Searching the heart: Women, men and romantic love in nineteenth-century America.* New York: Oxford University Press.

Macklin, E. D. (1972). Heterosexual cohabitation among unmarried students. *Family Coordinator, 21,* 463-472.

Makepeace, J. M. (1981). Courtship violence among college students. *Family Relations, 30,* 97-102.

Makepeace, J. M. (1983). Life events stress and courtship violence. *Family Relations, 32,* 101-109.

Makepeace, J. M. (1987). Social factors and victim-offender differences in courtship violence. *Family Relations, 36,* 87-91.

Malamuth, N. M. (1981). Rape proclivity among males. *Journal of Social Issues, 37*(4), 138-157.

Malone, J., Tyree, A., & O'Leary, K. D. (1989). Generalization and containment: Different effects of past aggression for wives and husbands. *Journal of Marriage and the Family, 51,* 687-698.

Margolis, M. L (1984). *Mothers and such: Views of American women and why they changed.* Los Angeles: University of California Press.

Markman, H. J. (1979). Application of a behavioral model of marriage in predicting relationship satisfaction of couples planning marriage. *Journal of Consulting and Clinical Psychology, 47,* 743-749.

Markman, H. J. (1981). Prediction of marital distress: A 5-year follow-up. *Journal of Consulting and Clinical Psychology, 49,* 760-762.

Markman, H. J. (1984). The longitudinal study of couples' interactions: Implications for understanding and predicting the development of marital distress. In K. Hahlweg & N. S. Jacobson, (Eds.), *Marital interaction* (pp. 253-281). New York: Guilford.

Markman, H. J., Floyd, F. J., Stanley, S. M., & Storaasli, R. D. (1988). Prevention of marital distress: A longitudinal investigation. *Journal of Personality and Social Psychology, 56,* 210-217.

Marshall, L. L., & Rose, P. (1987). Gender, stress and violence in the adult relationships of a sample of college students. *Journal of Social and Personal Relationships, 4,* 299-316.

Mason, A., & Blankenship, V. (1987). Power and affiliation motivation, stress and abuse in intimate relationships. *Journal of Personality and Social Psychology, 52,* 203-210.

Mayseless, O. (1991). Adult attachment patterns and courtship violence. *Family Relations, 40,* 21-28.

McCary, J. (1973). *Human sexuality: A brief edition.* New York: Van Nostrand.

McCornack, S. A., & Parks, M. R. (1990). What women know that men don't: Sex differences in determining the truth behind deceptive messages. *Journal of Social and Personal Relationships, 7,* 107-118.

Megli, J. M., & Morgan, L. G. (1991, May). *How to get a man and other advice: Articulation of the rhetorical visions present in popular women's magazines from 1974-1989.* Paper presented at the International Network Conference on Personal Relationships, Normal, IL.

Metts, S. (1989). An exploratory investigation of deception in close relationships. *Journal of Social and Personal Relationships, 6,* 159-179.

Milardo, R. M. (1982). Friendship networks in developing relationships: Converging and diverging social environments. *Social Psychology Quarterly, 45,* 162-172.

Miller, G. R., Mongeau, P. R., & Sleight, C. (1986). Fudging with friends and lying to lovers: Deceptive communication in personal relationships. *Journal of Social and Personal Relationships, 3,* 495-512.

Mintz, S., & Kellogg, S. (1988). *Domestic revolutions: A social history of American family life.* New York: Free Press.

Modell, J. (1983). Dating becomes the way of American youth. In D. Levine, L. P. Moch, L. A. Tilly, J. Modell, & E. Pleck, (Eds.), *Essays on the family and historical change* (pp. 169-175). College Station: Texas A & M University Press.

Modell, J. (1989). *Into one's own: From youth to adulthood in the United States: 1920-1975.* Berkeley: University of California Press.

Muehlenhard, C., & Cook, S. W. (1988). Men's self-reports of unwanted sexual activity. *The Journal of Sex Research, 24,* 58-72.

Muehlenhard, C. L. (1988). Misinterpreted dating behaviors and the risk of date rape. *Journal of Social and Clinical Psychology, 6,* 20-37.

Muehlenhard, C. L., & Linton, M. (1987). Date rape and sexual aggression in dating situations: Incidence and risk factors. *Journal of Counseling Psychology, 34,* 186-195.

Mueller, C., & Pope, H. (1977). Marital instability: A study of its transition between generations. *Journal of Marriage and the Family, 39,* 83-93.

Murstein, B. I. (1970). Stimulus-value-role: A theory of marital choice. *Journal of Marriage and the Family, 32,* 465-481.

Murstein, B. I. (1974). *Love, sex and marriage through the ages.* New York: Springer.

Murstein, B. I. (1976). *Who will marry whom?* New York: Springer.

Murstein, B. I. (1984). "Mate" selection in the year 2000. In L. A. Kirkendall & A. E. Gravatt (Eds.), *Marriage and family in the year 2020* (pp. 73-88). Buffalo: Prometheus.

Murstein, B. I. (1987). A clarification and extension of the SVR theory of dyadic pairing. *Journal of Marriage and the Family, 49,* 929-947.

Norton, A. J., & Glick, P. C. (1979). Marital instability in America: Past, present and future. In G. Levinger & C. Moles (Eds.), *Divorce and separation: Context, causes and consequences* (pp. 6-19). New York: Basic Books.

O'Keefe, N. K., Brockopp, K., & Chew, E. (1986). Teen dating violence. *Social Work, 31,* 465-468.

O'Leary, K. D., Barling, J., Arias, I., Rosenbaum, A., Malone, J., & Tyree, A. (1989). Prevalence and stability of physical aggression between spouses: A longitudinal analysis. *Journal of Consulting and Clinical Psychology, 57,* 263-268.

Parks, M. R., & Adelman, M. B. (1983). Communication networks and the development of romantic relationships: An expansion of uncertainty reduction theory. *Human Communication Research, 10,* 55-79.

Planalp, S., & Honeycutt, J. M. (1985). Events that increase uncertainty in personal relationships. *Human Communication Research, 11,* 593-604.

Pleck, E. (1987). *Domestic tyranny.* New York: Oxford University Press.

Price, R. A., & Vandenberg, S. S. (1979). Matching for physical attractiveness. *Personality and Social Psychology Bulletin, 5,* 398-400.

Prusank, D. T., Duran, R. L., & DeLillo, D. A. (1991, May). *Interpersonal relationships in women's magazines: Dating and relating in the 1970s and 1980s.* Paper presented at the International Network Conference on Personal Relationships, Normal, IL.

Reiss, I. L. (1960). Toward a sociology of the heterosexual love relationship. *Marriage and Family Living, 22,* 139-145.

Reiss, I. L. (1980). *Family Systems in America* (3rd ed.). New York: Holt, Rinehart & Winston.

Rice, F. P. (1990). *Intimate relationships, marriages and families.* Mountain View, CA: Mayfield.

Riggs, D. S., O'Leary, K. D., & Breslin, F. C. (1990). Multiple correlates of physical aggression in dating couples. *Journal of Interpersonal Violence, 5,* 61-73.

Robins, E., & Huston, T. L. (1983). *Testing compatibility testing.* Paper presented at the National Council on Family Relations Annual Meeting, St. Paul, MN.

Robins, E. J. (1983). *An empirical test of the compatibility testing model of marital choice.* Unpublished doctoral dissertation proposal, The Pennsylvania State University, State College.

Robins, E. J. (1985). *Compatibility, field search, and courtship progress: Examining the compatibility testing model of marital choice.* Unpublished manuscript, The University of North Carolina, Greensboro.

Robinson, I. E., & Jedlicka, D. (1982). Changes in sexual attitudes and behaviors of college students, 1965-1980: A research note. *Journal of Marriage and the Family, 43,* 77-83.

Roscoe, B., & Benaske, N. (1985). Courtship violence experienced by abused wives: Similarities in patterns of abuse. *Family Relations, 34,* 419-424.

Rothman, E. K. (1984). *Hands and hearts: A history of courtship in America.* New York: Basic Books.

Rubin, L. B. (1976). *Worlds of pain: Life in the working-class family.* New York: Basic Books.

Rubin, Z. (1970). Measurement of romantic love. *Journal of Personality and Social Psychology, 16,* 265-273.

Rubin, Z. (1973). *Liking and loving: An invitation to social psychology.* New York: Holt, Rinehart & Winston.

Rubin, Z., & Levinger, G. (1974). Theory and data badly mated: A critique of Murstein's SVR and Lewis's PDF models of mate selection. *Journal of Marriage and the Family, 36,* 226-231.

Rusbult, C. E. (1983). A longitudinal test of the investment model: The development (and deterioration) of satisfaction and commitment in heterosexual involvements. *Journal of Personality and Social Psychology, 45,* 101-117.

Rusbult, C. E., Johnson, D. J., & Morrow, G. D. (1986). Impact of couple patterns of problem solving on distress and nondistress in dating relationships. *Journal of Personality and Social Psychology, 50,* 744-753.

Russell, D. (1984). *Sexual exploitation.* Beverly Hills, CA: Sage.

Salholz, E., Michael, R., Starr, M., Doherty, S., Abramson, P., & Wingert, P. (1986, June 2). Too late for prince charming? *Newsweek,* pp. 54-61.

Schellenberg, J. A. (1960). Homogamy in personal values and the "field of eligibles." *Social Forces, 39,* 157-162.

Sears, R. R. (1977). Sources of life satisfaction of the Terman gifted men. *American Psychologist, 32,* 119-128.

Seward, R. (1978). *The American family: A demographic history.* Beverly Hills, CA: Sage.

Seyfried, B. A. (1977). Complementarity in interpersonal attraction. In S. W. Duck (Ed.), *Theory and practice in interpersonal attraction* (pp. 165-184). London: Academic Press.

Simpson, J. A. (1987). The dissolution of romantic relationships: Factors involved in relationship stability and emotional distress. *Journal of Personality and Social Psychology, 53,* 683-692.

Skolnick, A. S. (1987). *The intimate environment.* Boston: Little, Brown.

Smith-Rosenberg, C. (1985). *Disorderly conduct: Visions of gender in Victorian America.* New York: Oxford University Press.

Spanier, G. B. (1971). *A study of the relationship between and social correlates of romanticism and marital adjustment.* Unpublished master's thesis, Iowa State University.

Spanier, G. B. (1976). Measuring dyadic adjustment: New scales for assessing the quality of marriage and similar dyads. *Journal of Marriage and the Family, 38,* 15-28.

Sprecher, S. (1987). The effects of self disclosure given and received on affection for an intimate partner and stability of the relationship. *Journal of Social and Personal Relationships, 4,* 115-127.

Sprecher, S., & Femlee, D. (1991, August). *Effects of parents and friends on romantic relationships: A longitudinal investigation.* Paper presented at the American Sociological Association Annual Convention, Cincinnati, OH.

Stein, P. (1976). *Singleness.* Englewood Cliffs, NJ: Prentice-Hall.

Stephen, T. D. (1984a). A symbolic exchange framework for the development of intimate relationships. *Human Relations, 37,* 393-408.

Stephen, T. D. (1984b). Symbolic interdependence and post break-up distress: Reformulation of the attachment construct. *Journal of Divorce, 8,* 1-16.

Stephen, T. D. (1985). Fixed-sequence and circular-casual models of relationship development: Divergent views on the role of communication in intimacy. *Journal of Marriage and the Family, 47,* 955-963.

Sternberg, R. J. (1986). A triangular theory of love. *Psychological Review, 93,* 119-135.

Stets, J. E., & Henderson, D. A. (1991). Contextual factors surrounding conflict resolution while dating: Results from a national study. *Family Relations, 40,* 29-36.

Stets, J. E., & Pirog-Good, M. A. (1987). Violence in dating relationships. *Social Psychology Quarterly, 50,* 237-246.

Stets, J. E., & Pirog-Good, M. A. (1989). Patterns of physical and sexual abuse for men and women in dating relationships: A descriptive analysis. *Journal of Family Violence, 4,* 63-76.

Stets, J. E., & Pirog-Good, M. A. (1990). Interpersonal control and courtship aggression. *Journal of Social and Personal Relationships, 7,* 371-394.

Stewart, A. J., & Rubin, Z. (1974). The power motive in the dating couple. *Journal of Personality and Social Psychology, 34,* 305-309.

Stiles, H. R. (1871). *On bundling.* Mount Vernon, NY: Peter Pauper.

Sugarman, D. B., & Hotaling, G. T. (1989). Dating violence: Prevalence, context and risk markers. In M. Pirog-Good & J. Stets (Eds.), *Violence in dating relationships* (pp. 3-32). New York: Praeger.

Surra, C. A. (1985). Courtship types: Variations in interdependence between partners and social networks. *Journal of Personality and Social Psychology, 56*, 357-375.

Surra, C. A. (1987). Reasons for changes in commitment: Variations by courtship style. *Journal of Social and Personal Relationships, 4*, 17-33.

Surra, C. A. (1990). Research and theory on mate selection and premarital relationships in the 1980s. *Journal of Marriage and the Family, 52*, 844-865.

Surra, C. A., Arizzi, P., & Asmussen, L. L. (1988). The association between reasons for commitment and the development and outcome of marital relationships. *Journal of Social and Personal Relationships, 5*, 47-63.

Surra, C. A., & Longstreth, M. (1990). Similarity of outcomes, interdependence, and conflict in dating relationships. *Journal of Personality and Social Psychology, 59*, 1-16.

Terman, L. M. (1938). *Psychological factors in marital happiness.* New York: McGraw-Hill.

Terman, L. M., & Buttenweiser, P. (1938). Personality factors in marital compatibility. *Journal of Social Psychology, 6*, 143-171.

Terman, L. M., & Oden, M. H. (1947). *The gifted child grows up.* Stanford, CA: Stanford University Press.

Tharp, R. G. (1963). Psychological patterning in marriage. *Psychological Bulletin, 60*, 97-117.

Thibaut, J. W., & Kelley, H. H. (1959). *The social psychology of groups.* New York: John Wiley.

Tibbits, C. (1965). The older family member in American society. In H. Jacobs (Ed.), *The older person in the family: Challenges and conflicts* (pp. 1-11). Iowa City, IA: The Institute of Gerontology.

Tolhuizen, J. H. (1991, May). *Issues of deception in dating relationships.* Paper presented at the International Network Conference on Personal Relationships, Normal, IL.

Tucker, L. R. (1966). Learning theory and multivariate experiment: Illustration by determination of generalized learning curves. In R. Cattell (Ed.), *Handbook of multivariate experimental psychology* (pp. 476-501). Chicago: Rand McNally.

Vaillant, G. E. (1978). Natural history of male psychological health: VI. Correlates of successful marriage and fatherhood. *American Journal of Psychiatry, 135*, 653-659.

Waller, W. (1937). The rating and dating complex. *American Sociological Review, 2*, 727-734.

Waller, W. (1951). *The family: A dynamic interpretation.* New York: Dryden.

Walster, E., Aronson, V., Abrahams, D., & Rottman, L. (1966). Importance of physical attractiveness in dating behavior. *Journal of Personality and Social Psychology, 4*, 508-516.

Walster, E. H., Walster, G. W., & Berscheid, E. (1978). *Equity theory and research.* Boston: Allyn & Bacon.

Walster, E. H., Walster, G. W., & Traupmann, J. (1978). Equity and premarital sex. *Journal of Personality and Social Psychology, 36,* 82-92.

Wamboldt, F. S., & Reiss, D. (1989). Defining a family heritage and a new relationship: Two central themes in the making of a marriage. *Family Process, 28,* 317-335.

Watson, D., & Clark, L. A. (1984). Negative affectivity: The disposition to experience aversive emotional states. *Psychological Bulletin, 96,* 465-490.

Watson, J. D. (1927, March 6). *Chicago Tribune,* p. 1.

White, L. K. (1990). Determinants of Divorce: A review of research in the eighties. *Journal of Marriage and the Family, 52,* 904-912.

Winch, R. F. (1955a). The theory of complementary needs in mate selection: A test of one kind of complementariness. *American Sociological Review, 20,* 52-56.

Winch, R. F. (1955b). The theory of complementary needs in mate selection: Final results on the test of the general hypothesis. *American Sociological Review, 20,* 552-555.

Winch, R. F., Ktsanes, T., & Ktsanes, V. (1954). The theory of complementary needs in mate selection: An analytic and descriptive study. *American Sociological Review, 19,* 241-249.

Wolfe, L. (1981). *The cosmo report.* New York: Ann Arbor House.

Zelnick, M., & Kanter, J. (1980). Sexual activity, contraceptive use and pregnancy among metropolitan-area teenagers. *Family Planning Perspectives, 12,* 230.

Index

About the Authors

Rodney M. Cate is Associate Dean for Research and Graduate Education in the College of Family and Consumer Sciences at Iowa State University. He is also Professor of Family Studies in the Department of Human Development and Family Studies. Prior to his present position, he was on the faculty at Washington State University, Oregon State University, and Texas Tech University for 12 years. He is currently a co-principal investigator on a longitudinal study of the effect of deployment of a spouse to Operation Desert Storm on families and children, funded by the National Institute of Mental Health. He has received the James M. Moran Memorial Research Award given by the American Home Economics Association Foundation for career research contributions in the area of children and families. He has published numerous manuscripts in family studies, social psychology, and interdisciplinary oriented journals. He also has co-authored a chapter on courtship in Duck's *Handbook of Personal*

Relationships. His current research interests are in the areas of premarital relationship development, abusive premarital relationships, and social cognition in developing relationships. He is involved in such organizations as the International Society for the Study of Personal Relationships (presently on the Board of Directors), the International Network on Personal Relationships, the National Council on Family Relations, and the American Psychological Association.

Sally A. Lloyd has been Professor and Chair of Family and Consumer Sciences at Miami University, Oxford, Ohio since 1990. Prior to this she was on the faculty at the University of Utah. Her research centers on courtship, particularly the dissolution of relationships, and violence in courtship and marriage. She has published extensively in family studies, social psychology, and other interdisciplinary journals. She is also a coauthor with Rodney Cate for a chapter on courtship in Duck's *Handbook of Personal Relationships*. Currently she is working on a longitudinal study of violence and everyday marital interaction that was funded by the Harry Frank Guggenheim Foundation.